Sow Simple

SOW SIMPLE

100+ Green and Easy Projects to Make Your Garden Awesome

CHRISTINA SYMONS & JOHN GILLESPIE

HARBOUR PUBLISHING CO. LTD.

1 2 3 4 5 — 16 15 14 13 12

Harbour Publishing Co. Ltd.
P.O. Box 219, Madeira Park, BC, V0N 2H0
www.harbourpublishing.com

Edited by Carol Pope
Cover and text design by Five Seventeen/PicaPica.ca
Printed and bound in China through Colorcraft Ltd., Hong Kong

Harbour Publishing acknowledges financial support from the Government of Canada through the Canada Book Fund
and the Canada Council for the Arts, and from the Province of British Columbia through the BC Arts Council
and the Book Publishing Tax Credit.

LIBRARY AND ARCHIVES CANADA CATALOGUING IN PUBLICATION

Symons, Christina
Sow simple : 100+ green and easy projects to make your
garden awesome / Christina Symons and John Gillespie.

Includes index.
ISBN 978-1-55017-574-5

1. Gardening.
2. Nature craft.
I. Gillespie, John, 1964–
II. Title.

SB453.S96 2012   635   C2012-900321-2

ACKNOWLEDGEMENTS

We would like to thank Harbour Publishing for their continued support of our work and for the
opportunity to publish our second book with their very talented team, including awesome designer,
Five Seventeen. Our astute and kind editor, Carol Pope, calmly and creatively organized a mountain of
ideas, tips and tricks into a coherent collection, step by step. For this we are very grateful. Every garden
we get to work on is a gift and we thank John's Landwise Consulting clients, colleagues and team for
those amazing opportunities. In a similar way, we also appreciate the editorial and commercial writing
and photography assignments which inspire us and allow us to share our work with the world. Our
sweet parents, partners, family and friends support us in endless ways and we pay them back by offering
experimental cocktails, very large zucchinis and odd-looking orphan shrubs. We love you guys very
much. Just remember, plant it with the green side up! With gratitude, J+C

For our friends and family—
may you always have seeds
in your pockets.

In memory of Cliff.

DIG IN

GET GROWING

NO RULES

DESIGN WISE

GOOD TIMES

PREFACE

It really is sow simple. Starting from the ground up with a "no rules" gardening philosophy that honours the ancient wisdom of our earth, landscape designer John Gillespie and lifestyle writer-photographer Christina Symons share how easy it can be to live in paradise.

Using unfussy and often repurposed materials and taking a straightforward step-by-step approach, *Sow Simple: 100+ Easy Tips and Projects to Make Your Garden Awesome* is the ultimate earthwise guide for any green thumb—urban or rural, new or knowledgeable. Using strategies deeply rooted in a respect for nature's balance, John and Christina have coaxed an inspired ecological respite—an Everyday Eden—out of their small bit of back forty. Digging in joyously, they have learned that a garden is integral to a full and happy life.

In John and Christina's garden, organic edibles burst from the earth all year round—from springtime through winter in blanketed beds and in quick cloches and rigged-up row covers. Tough-love trios of edible alliums add architectural interest and insect resistance, seeds are saved, herbs harvested, berries loaded into buckets, portable potagers planted and tabletop salad snipped. Bare-root trees burst into fruit and foliage for a four-season tapestry of blossom and beauty. Vines become vino, apples turn into elixir, edible petals are plucked, sun tea and rhubarb lemonade served up, figs and olives harvested, asparagus stalks skewered, fruit grilled, peppers dished up red-hot and pumpkins scooped for soup. Children are wowed with garden-fresh flavours, then charmed by solar photos, sunflower feeders, botanical prints and leafy impressions.

Plants abound thanks to John's easy approach to propagation, tired shrubs are renewed and compost heats up new roots. Where pollination is slow, Mother Nature is given a nudge. Favourable fungus, beneficial bugs, magical mulches, edible weeds, water-wise wildflowers and native plantings are all welcomed. Plants are trialed and audited, the art of fertilization is demystified, weeding is tamed, and lawn and order is sensibly restored. Transplanting is made easy, and the move of a garden smoothed with back-sparing and time-thrifty techniques. Dogs and kitties are directed to pet-friendly patches, deer and rabbits gently discouraged and plant pests arrested in earth-savvy ways.

And nothing is wasted. Old boots and rickety boats are stuffed with succulents, cracked tiles are layered onto a mosaic masterpiece, secondhand dishes become windowsill adornments, stumps are hollowed to house sedums and just about everything imaginable is planted up. In fact, beauty shines out in every corner. Christina's hanging baskets brim with blooming bulbs while handmade pot trellises show off flowering vines. Easy edgings add structure, and John's no-fear shear strategy keeps even unruly trees and hedgings perfectly pruned.

Design wise, ideas abound. A living gate makes a spectacular entrance and flagstone feels good underfoot. Home-crafted concrete troughs stuffed with succulents stand strong alongside dry-stack stone walls. Terra cotta adds a sense of Tuscany, stone is supremo, courtyards are courted and John and Christina go to the wall with vertical and rooftop gardens. Water gardens and sweet touches add whimsy, while playhouses, gazebos, garden groves, tiki bars and backyard benches proliferate.

And throughout the year, there is gratitude and ongoing celebration—branch bouquets, ice candles, cool yuletide displays, flower shooters, fruit cubes and berry swizzles—all harvest-inspired affirmations of what the good life can really mean when you live it in a garden.

—Carol Pope

INTRODUCTION

You know, the longer we garden, the more we realize how essential it is for a full and happy life. No matter how stressful a typical day becomes, if it starts and ends with a pinch of mint or something special from our garden, chances are we can go to bed with thanks and a smile—and wake up the next day similarly inspired!

When we first started gardening in a big way, we were studying formal horticulture (John) and herbology (Christina). The texts we read back then felt more like rules and regulations containing stiff information about design fundamentals and proper gardening techniques, hardiness zones, Latin names, historic uses and the like. It was all very intimidating and frankly felt a little overwhelming. We wondered if gardening as a day-to-day passion or vocation really had to be so complicated. All of these technical terms and practices do have their place, of course, but our love for gardening felt light, curious and happy—not heavy in any way!

And so we carried on, with open hearts and wide eyes, curiosity as our guide. We set off more like horticultural explorers, collecting ideas and inspiration, while conducting experiments in every patch and around every corner.

Along the way, we discovered that gardening is not so complicated after all.

John is naturally inclined to go rogue in the garden, testing rules and pushing the edges (literally and figuratively) of garden design, installation and maintenance. Christina prefers to craft and cook and contemplate the bounty and beauty in amongst small pleasures and simple details. For us, making something out of nothing and eating from the garden used to be partly a financial necessity, now it's simply a challenge and joy in tune with healthy living and contemporary ecology (which also saves us money!).

Today, people often stop by our garden—our very quirky piece of paradise—and ask about this, that and the other project, plant or installation. The more experienced gardeners are sometimes skeptical about our various experiments—"You *can't* grow wine grapes like that," they say bluntly, in response to a snaky new trellis in front of a hedge. And our response is likely to be "Well let's bet—a bottle of merlot?—you're on!" Win or lose, it's all good fun to us.

In *Sow Simple*, we've pulled together some of our favourite tips, tricks and projects for you to have a go with in the garden. There's a wealth of practical, proven advice to apply whenever you are in need of a fresh, easy approach to your everyday gardening chores. Consider the special projects and recipes as little pick-me-ups, designed to add a layer of delight to your garden and outdoor spaces. And, we promise, nothing is overly complicated.

We hope you will roll up your sleeves and take the simpler approach with us. Because gardening (much like life) is messy, informal and imperfect, but with the right attitude, it can also be a total blast.

xo Christina + John

everydayeden.com

DIG IN

Let's get this party started! Wondering where to begin in your garden? Us too! There is always something to do, a new bed to plan, a new plant to discover. The best way to start is to just dig in, set a few simple goals and create a solid base of plantings—trees, shrubs, open spaces and edges—to build the framework for the soul of your garden to emerge over time. Of course, it never hurts to break up those bigger chores with a few fast and easy projects. Consider them the exclamation points for the story that's about to unfold.

SWEET TREATS

Silver pots of mini daffs make great gifts. So easy and sweet. They will also look adorable on your own windowsill.

1 Look for old silver sugar bowls and creamers at the thrift store. Using a hammer and a big nail, pop a few holes in each of the bottoms.

2 Then carefully split one pot of flowering daffodils between three small containers.

3 Plant them up with a bit of potting soil. Collect a titch of moss, pebbles or mulch from your garden to blanket the top and hold the stems in place.

MATERIALS

Secondhand silver sugar bowls or creamers from your local thrift store

Hammer and large nail

One pot of flowering daffodils

Potting soil

PORTABLE POTAGER

MATERIALS

10-gallon pot or a two-handled
yard-cleanup bucket

Hammer and large nail, or drill, to add
drainage holes if needed

Selection of edible bedding
plants and/or seeds

Optional, for a climbing-plant trellis:

Two bamboo poles

Bamboo cane

Screws

Wire

Chicken wire

A garden, a garden—what I would give for a garden! This is the song of the apartment dweller in spring, the senior in a retirement home, the urban professional with very little time. But you don't need an expansive plot of land to have your own mini Eden. A portable potager—or mini-kitchen garden—is the answer. You can make it in a day, move it around your balcony or patio, and reap a tidy harvest from this humble plot.

1 Locate a 10-gallon pot. (Large-specimen trees come in these sturdy plastic containers, so you might wish to ask your local nursery or landscaper to give you a used one.) Other options include two-handled plastic yard buckets (handy but you must drill drainage holes) or large decorative plastic pots. Avoid heavy ceramic containers unless you plan to keep your potager in one place only.

2 Create a simple trellis for peas and beans using two bamboo poles, with a bamboo cane as a horizontal support. Secure with screws and wire, then hang chicken wire from cane to pot (fold it over the support and bury into the soil or secure to edge of pot).

3 In this simple pot you can grow 15–20 pea plants, 2–3 strawberries, 2–3 Swiss chards, some edible flowers such as nasturtium and calendula and a pair of squash or cucumber. Grow the peas on the front of the trellis and the squash up the back. By the time the peas are finished, the squash will be ready to take over.

4 Enjoy your piece of potted paradise!

Recycled wire hanging basket

Potting soil

Moss if you have a sustainable source, or coir (coconut fibre)

Selection of spring-flowering bulbs

BULB BASKET

No room for bulbs in your garden? Recycle your summer hanging basket into a bulb showpiece for spring.

1 Remove any spent flowers and plant material from your summer hanging baskets. Replenish soil as needed.

2 Next, plant a generous assortment of larger bulbs such as narcissus, tulip and hyacinth throughout the top section of the basket. Cover with a layer of moss (from a sustainable source in your yard) or coir.

3 Tuck in smaller bulbs such as crocuses and snowdrops into the sides of the basket and to fill any empty spaces on top.

4 Store your bulb basket in a cool, protected space throughout the winter, such as under a deck or in your garden shed. In cold climates, you can also dig a hole and sink it into the ground, or store in an unheated, insulated crawlspace.

5 In early spring (or when temperatures in your area are consistently above freezing), hang your basket outdoors in a sunny spot.

6 Water and watch the show!

GO FOR BROKE

Here is the ultimate way to recycle broken dishes and cracked pottery—use them to turn a simple wooden planter into a mosaic masterpiece.

MATERIALS

One sturdy, flat-sided wooden planter box

Broken or cracked ceramic dishes, tiles or terra cotta

Mallet and cloth cover (if needed for breaking)

Sanded tile grout

Tile-grout sealer (optional)

Gloves

Trowel

Rags

1 Gather your collection of broken ceramic dishes, tiles or terra cotta. Or, break pieces on a hard surface using a mallet and a cloth cover for protection.

2 Practise laying out a design on your planter to test the fit and to be sure you have enough mosaic pieces to cover the entire surface.

3 Mix your tile grout according to package directions and apply a thick layer to the surface of your planter. Wearing gloves to protect your hands, press pieces into the grout, allowing the excess to ooze out between them. Create patterns and designs or arrange randomly. Smooth the grout and be sure that the entire surface of your box is covered either by tile or grout.

TIP: Use odd pieces like broken cups to create funky touches that you can pot up.

4 Once the pieces are all attached, wipe off excess grout and allow it to cure slightly for 30 minutes to an hour. Next, use a wet cloth to smooth surfaces and remove remaining grout from your mosaic pieces. Fill in any gaps with extra grout. After the grout has cured completely, tile-grout sealer may be applied for extra protection.

5 Plant up your mosaic planter and enjoy!

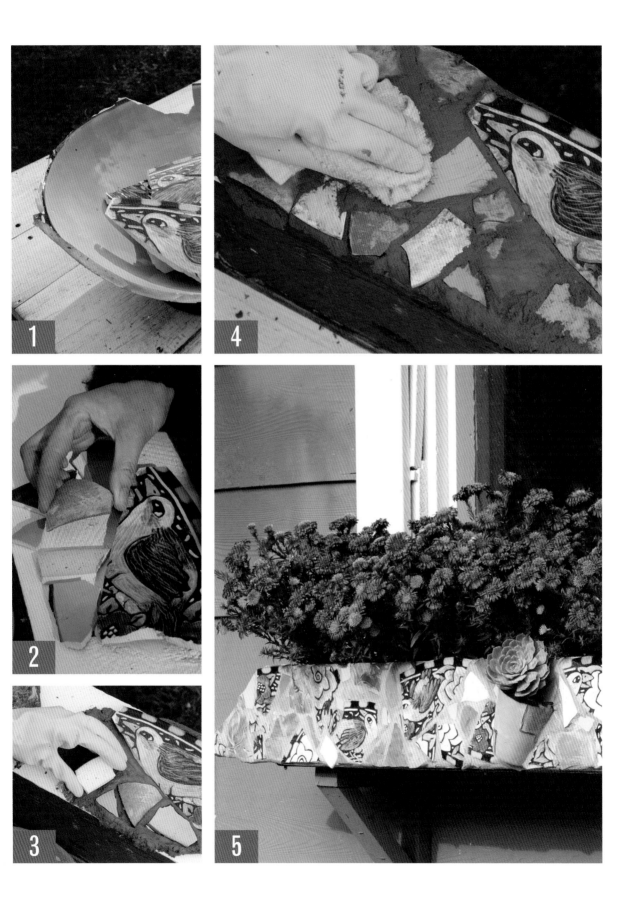

MATERIALS

A pair of similarly shaped moulds, one
25 percent smaller than the other

Concrete ready mix

Organic matter (for hypertufa):
peat moss, cocoa husks, wood
chips or sawdust

Rubber gloves

Nonstick cooking spray
(for plastic moulds)

Plastic lining (for cardboard moulds)

Sticks to create drainage holes

Water

QUIRKY CONCRETE CONTAINERS

*Concrete planters and hypertufa troughs are easier
to make than you might think. The only difference:
one is smooth (concrete) and one is rustic and
rough (hypertufa).*

1 First, decide on a shape. Squat shapes are easiest for beginners
and make wonderful troughs and low bowls for succulents and
other plants typically grown in rocky areas.

2 Create a pair of moulds (inside and outside) by selecting or
fashioning two identical shapes, one approximately 25 percent
smaller than the other. For example, two plastic bowls in similar
shapes that fit inside each other with a little more than an inch
(about 3 cm) space between them. Cardboard boxes also work
well. Spray plastic containers with nonstick cooking spray. If
using cardboard, line your moulds with plastic.

3   Mix your concrete according to package directions. To create a hypertufa blend, add approximately 30 percent peat moss, cocoa husks, wood chips or sawdust to the mix prior to adding water. This will result in a stiffer mix. A plain concrete mix will not be as rigid.

4   Fill the bottom and sides of your moulds with your mix of choice to a thickness of 1½ in. (4 cm). Insert lengths of sticks cut the same depth as your mix to create drainage holes.

5   Place your inner mould on top. Press down until the bottom and sides are of an even thickness. Position stones or other weights inside the top mould to hold it down. Tap the mould several times to remove air bubbles.

6   Allow your pot or trough to dry for several days. Then release the concrete from the moulds and remove drainage sticks. Allow the containers to cure, preferably outside where rain can wash over them for several weeks before planting.

MATERIALS

Stone as required

Removable landscape
paint, rope or hoses

Shovel or fork

String line

ROCK ON!

In the English countryside, alongside miles of lovely hedgerows, centuries-old rock walls weave across the landscape like a gardener's signature from the past. They were built simply with gathered stone, stacked in defining lines to indicate property borders, keep livestock in or out and delineate field crops.

But sometime around the 1950s, traditional dry-stack rock walls (those without mortar) fell out of fashion, especially in North American gardens. Instead we embraced the promise of perfection and began hardscaping with zeal, fashioning retaining walls and other garden structures of smooth, impermeable and permanent concrete.

But trends, like concrete, eventually shift and crack. Today dry-stack rock walls are beginning to resurface in the garden world. For hardscaping beginners, this is a wonderful development, as there is no easier way to build a sturdy defining garden wall than to simply stack stone.

No stone wall is exactly the same as the next, and each stone crafter will develop his or her unique technique and style. Over time, nature, humans and animals will impact whatever "perfection" the wall crafter was able to achieve. Walls may crumble, slump and become overgrown—this is simply the unique character of dry-stack stone.

1 To build a rock wall around a garden bed, first select and collect the appropriate type of stone. Immense walls or those that need to carry strong retaining features are best suited to large, quarried stone. You can purchase quarried stone for retaining walls at a commercial quarry or landscape-supply store. Smaller rock walls or garden-bed walls may be fashioned from field stone, small angular or square-cut stones, river rock or cobblestone. You can also use a mixture of stone shapes for a natural-looking wall that offers the most flexibility during construction. Deciding how much stone to purchase or collect is difficult, so you may wish to build your wall in stages. As a general rule, having more stone on hand is better as it gives you a broader choice to select from.

2 Define your wall's layout—use removable landscape paint, rope or hoses to mark the shape of your wall against the ground. Before you build, step back and take a look at the outline from as many angles as possible. Once you are satisfied, you can begin to build.

3 Use large stones to give definition to the wall and provide strength, then small stones to easily fill in the gaps and soften shapes. Start with the large foundation stones and use a shovel or fork to dig out spaces along your wall's layout line. Rock and roll your foundation stones into place using braces to obtain leverage. Once your foundation stones are in place, begin stacking and filling with other smaller stones in a crisscross fashion to ensure strength and avoid toppling.

4 Backfill the spaces behind the wall to make it stronger. Keep the front of your wall flat by positioning the stones accordingly with their flat sides outward. Step back often to check your work and ensure the sides of your walls are approximately level. You can also use a string line to check the height and sides.

Why We Love Dry-Stack Rock Walls and Features

Dry-stack rock walls offer numerous benefits for insects and wildlife, such as providing habitat for squirrels and snakes.

Unlike concrete, dry-stacking allows water to percolate and return naturally to the water table.

The spaces between the stones are natural planting places.

And, because the rocks are not contained by mortar, you can tear down and move your wall in the future, should you have a change of heart.

DOG-GONE PURR-FECT GARDEN

Family pets add so much joy to our hectic lives but they can sometimes wreak havoc in the garden. While it's heart-lifting to get a friendly wag or soft nuzzle during gardening chores, it's not so sweet to come across a steaming lump of kitty "scat" in a newly planted carrot patch. Or, imagine that the unusual lily bulb you've just unearthed is really Rover's rotting bone! Here's how to design a Fido-friendly garden with some specific no-pet zones.

MOVE OVER, ROVER. Cats and dogs find newly worked soil irresistible—it's like a fresh and fluffy litter box ready for digging and deposits. Keeping your cat or dog away from the just-planted plots will spare everyone some grief.

SCAT, CAT! Add a topcoat of textured mulch such as composted straw, pine cones, leaf mould or composted wood chips to dissuade your cat and dog from diving in. Cats particularly have a delicate disposition and don't like anything rough or unstable beneath their feet. Delicate seed plots may also be protected by barriers such as a temporary cloak of chicken wire or a rigged-up hoop house until seedlings are established. Spiky shrub branches or thorny rose clippings can also keep pets away.

MAKE SCENTS. Use pungent herbs such as lemon thyme or balm, lavender and rue to deter cats and dogs. The scent of citronella and citrus peels are also reported to repel kitty, as is *Coleus canina*—also called the "scaredy-cat plant."

ENGAGE WATER POWER. More serious pet problems may be curtailed by a sprinkler activated by motion. Over time, the surprise spray will teach your dog or cat to select another spot to scrutinize.

CREATE BOUNDARIES. Fencing a garden will naturally keep dogs at bay but may not prevent cats from getting in. To make your fence less feline friendly, install a line of plastic or string at the top—essentially anything that makes the surface feel flimsy to furry little feet.

PROVIDE A SPOT FOR SPOT. Add a pet-friendly place where your dog is welcome to lie down and view "his territory."

CREATE KITTY CORNERS. Plant catnip (*Nepeta* × *faassenii*, *N. cataria*) wherever you would like your cat to prowl and play. Other feline-favoured picks are lemon grass, oat grass, sweet grass and wheat grass—all of which your kitty will love to chew.

AVOID CHEMICAL WARFARE. Never use such deterrents as burying mothballs in your garden to dissuade digging. Mothballs are toxic. Likewise, lawn and garden herbicides and pesticides can be deadly to pets who pick up chemicals on their paws and then lick them clean. Animals can also track toxins into your home, exposing you and your family.

DON'T TEACH YOUR OLD (OR YOUNG) DOG NEW TRICKS. At least, not if you will regret it later. A "one-time" game of toss with a damaged zucchini now has our dog convinced it's clever to chomp on squash and cucumbers.

CONSIDER ALL CREATURES. To ensure that your patch is secure for all its inhabitants, attach a tiny bell to your pet's collar. Now your backyard's bliss will extend to visiting birds as well as to your furry family members.

MATERIALS

Spade or shovel

Compost, manure, topsoil and aged woodchips

Sand

Water

Mulch

PLANTING 101

As gardeners, we spend a lot of time researching the perfect plants, then locating, pruning and fertilizing them. But often we neglect to put the same investment into the actual planting! Giving your plant a good start will pay enormous dividends over the years and is one of the key ways to ensure your garden reaches great expectations.

1 Start with well-rooted stock. If the plant is pot-bound when you remove the container, vertically slice the roots with a shovel or spade and cut or remove any larger girdled roots. Strip off all strings from ball-and-burlap plants and fold or pull away the burlap if the roots are well developed. Break the rim off biodegradable containers and slice the sides.

2 Be sure to place your plant in the garden at the same soil depth as it was in its original container. The planting hole should be as wide as possible. Expend your energy going sideways rather than deep. A broad square hole is actually better than a "perfect" pot-like space, allowing roots more room to spread out without wrapping around the rootball.

3 Saturate the hole. Fill it with water several times before planting and final backfilling.

4 Place your plant. Use plenty of backfill to fill the hole. Compost, manure, topsoil and aged woodchips, along with a shovelful of sand, will help to keep soil loose and allow roots to get a good start. Most of the soil's available nutrients, beneficial organisms and water are near the surface. If you are in an area that has wet clay soils, look for plants that prefer these conditions or dig a wide and shallow hole to encourage horizontal root growth. By allowing the plant to spread its roots near the surface, you can avoid having it sit in a bathtub-like situation that will be too wet.

5 Create a ring of mulch around the plant so that a shallow "trench" encircles the trunk. This will ensure that water soaks into the roots rather than just running off during times of drought.

MATERIALS

Bare-root tree(s)

Burlap sack or tarp

Tub of water

Shovel

An equal mix of aged wood chips, composted manure or compost

1–2 shovelfuls sand

Tree guard

Stake (optional)

BARE SEASON

In early spring, it's always entertaining to see excited gardeners with large shrubs and trees strapped to car rooftops or poking out of sunroofs. Many of these newly acquired plants are difficult to lift, transport and extract from their containers for replanting. The answer? Bare roots! In late winter and early spring you can often purchase plants without any soil—a very sensible option if you know how to care for them from the get-go.

1 Protect your plant's exposed roots—when purchasing, ask for a bag or cover them with a tarp or burlap sack. Once you arrive home, soak your specimen's roots in a tub of water out of the sun until you are able to plant—do not rely on rain to give your plant enough moisture. Plant as soon as possible.

2 Dig the hole one third wider and approximately the same depth as the root mass. Place the tree and spread the roots outwards You'll need a good growing medium to fill your hole—this is vital for a successful start of soil-less roots. An equal mix of aged wood chips, composted manure or regular compost works well. A healthy portion of sand (1–2 shovelfuls) also encourages proper root development.

3 Backfill the hole and, on fruit trees especially, watch for graft points (the place where rootstock connects to the trunk) and do not bury this area beneath your soil. Use a simple tree guard around the base (we make ours from circles of repurposed carpet with a hole cut for the trunk) to prevent weed-eater damage or, better yet, add a healthy portion of mulch to keep weeds away from your new planting.

4 For taller bare-root plants, staking may be required for the first year or until roots can firmly establish themselves. To stake a tree, select a sturdy wooden or metal stake approximately 5 ft. (1.5 m) tall. Dull the top of the stake with a rubber topper or by smoothing the surface of the wood. Pound the stake into the soil, approximately 1 ft. (30 cm) from the tree trunk. In windy areas, use 3 stakes positioned an equal distance apart around the tree. Angle the stakes away from the tree for added strength. Use a cable or rope tied to the end of the stake and around the tree. Protect the tree trunk from tension damage with a piece of cloth or rubber hose. Once the tree is established after several seasons, remove the stake(s).

L–R: STRAWBERRY TREE FRUIT, *Arbutus unedo*; GIANT SEQUOIA, *Sequoiadendron giganteum*; MAIDENHAIR TREE, *Ginkgo biloba*

TREES PLEASE

Trees signify largely in our lives and environments. Noteworthy in landscapes and memories, they shade and shelter us—and remind us of childhood tree forts and swings, of revolving seasons of blossom and beauty.

The best planting times for trees are spring and fall. Once in the ground, be sure to add plenty of organic material and use mulch to create a well around the tree for watering. Keep the mulch at least 6 in. (15 cm) away from the trunk. Ensuring your tree receives adequate water for the first couple of years should be your prime concern after you have planted it.

Planting the right tree in the right place is your best key to success. Do your research, shop around and ask questions. Not sure what to plant? As a place to start, here are 10 wonderful trees guaranteed to provide you with some beautiful memories.

1 JAPANESE STEWARTIA (*STEWARTIA PSEUDOCAMELLIA*). There are far too few of these lovely small trees (30 ft./9 m at maturity), with their wonderful fall colours, gorgeously mottled bark and camellia-like white flowers.

2 GIANT DOGWOOD (*CORNUS CONTROVERSA*). Exquisite with a typically layered or tiered branching habit, white flowers and showy fruits.

3 SOURWOOD (*OXYDENDRUM ARBOREUM*). Although this small tree boasts fragrant clusters of white flowers, the autumn colours are the top highlight for many.

4 ANTARCTIC BEECH (*NOTHOFAGUS ANTARCTICA*). Recently we had the pleasure of visiting an inspiring garden with a grove of these Southern Hemisphere trees—their knarled and mossy trunks were like works of sculpture!

5 MEDLAR (*MESPILUS GERMANICA*). Medlar's apple-like fruit is edible after a frost and yet this appealing small tree (that grows to 20 ft./6 m) is rarely cultivated.

6 DAWN REDWOOD (*METASEQUOIA GLYPTOSTROBOIDES*). Discovered in 1941, this living fossil with a distinctive buttressed trunk is a deciduous conifer of unknown heights. Tough enough for almost any situation.

7 GIANT SEQUOIA OR SIERRA REDWOOD (*SEQUOIADENDRON GIGANTEUM*). Looking way up, you will see a very robust-looking conical tree. Its spongy, thick and fissured bark is resistant to fire and looks great in a grove.

8 MAIDENHAIR TREE (*GINKGO BILOBA*). *Ginkgo* is Japanese for "silver fruit," while *biloba* refers to the two-lobed leaf. Frequently it is called maidenhair because of a similarity in foliage to maidenhair fern. Ginkgo is a sight to see in the autumn, when leaves turn vivid gold.

9 STRAWBERRY TREE (*ARBUTUS UNEDO*). This very picturesque, 20-ft. (6-m) evergreen from Turkey and Lebanon closely resembles our own local arbutus. While native arbutus can be challenging to establish, the strawberry tree is extremely tough and resistant to disease. Compact shrub forms are also available.

10 WOLLEMI PINE (*WOLLEMIA NOBILIS*). For something different, search for a specimen of this ancient wonder. The mysterious Wollemi pine was unknown until 1994, when it was discovered in a deep canyon in Wollemi National Park near Sydney, Australia.

Shrub border includes smoke bush, *Cotinus coggygria* 'Royal Purple'; potentilla, *Potentilla fruticosa*; shrub rose, *Rosa rugosa*; English lavender, *Lavandula angustifolia* 'Munstead'.

Opposite: California lilac (*Ceanothus* spp.)

SHRUB IT UP

In the landscape industry, there's a saying when you need to make a garden happen quickly: "shrub it up!" Shrubs are much smaller than trees yet more robust than perennials. Their bark, flowers, fruits, foliage and seasonal colour provide instant and year-round interest.

Shrubs contribute body and texture to the garden and are low maintenance if properly chosen. For best results, choose your shrubs by thinking about your locale. Conditions to consider include the shrub's water, sun/shade and soil requirements. This selection is a great starting point in your search for a perfect showing of shrubs.

1 **HIGHBUSH BLUEBERRY (*VACCINIUM CORYMBOSUM*).** All gardens should include as many edible plants as possible. This foot-high North American native plant has nice structure and is easy to care for. It features great ornamental foliage and autumn red/yellow colour, beautiful white and sometimes pink-tinged flowers and, of course, sweet blueberries. Many cultivars have been selected over the years and the range of fruit production can be spread over the summer and early fall by carefully selecting early-, mid- and late-season cultivars.

2 MINT BUSH (*PROSTANTHERA CUNEATA* AND *P. ROTUNDIFOLIA*). A bushy, waist-high shrub with a minty aroma when leaves are rubbed, the Australian mint bush is a perfect choice for a fragrant garden. Not susceptible to harsh climatic conditions, this Australian native is at ease in many challenging sites but will do best in a sheltered, sunny spot.

3 ESCALLONIA (*ESCALLONIA* SPP.). This shrub is a no-nonsense, tough and consistent specimen that grows well in a variety of challenging situations, reaching a height of about 5 ft. (1.5 m). A proven and efficient evergreen with bright, long-flowering, pink-red flowers, it will often continue to bloom far into fall. Planted in full sun, it works well in seaside settings. Escallonia also makes a great choice for an informal flowering hedge.

4 CALIFORNIA LILAC (*CEANOTHUS* SPP.). Cultivars and species such as *Ceanothus* 'Concha' and *C. gloriosus* (Point Reyes creeper) offer deep-blue flowers along arching and dense stalks. Originating from western North America and Mexico, these sturdy evergreen beauties range from ground huggers to large shrubs and are at home in rockeries and parking-lot plantings.

5 TREE ANEMONE (*CARPENTERIA CALIFORNICA*). With glossy, deep-green leathery leaves, the tree anemone's sweetly fragrant cup-shaped yellow flowers are worthy of our attention. Little pruning is required for this California native that grows up to about 8 ft. (2.4 m) tall.

6 SILK TASSEL BUSH (*GARRYA ELLIPTICA*). The large silk tassel bush has unique, wavy-edged and glossy green leaves. During winter and spring it produces grey-green male catkins that hang down. Very low maintenance, this hearty shrub reaches up to 10 ft. (3 m) and will give your garden a solid foundation.

+ Other honourable mentions when it comes to favourite shrubs are rosemary (*Rosmarinus officinalis*), purple leaf barberry (*Berberis thunbergii*), evergreen huckleberry (*Vaccinium ovatum*), sun rose (*Helianthemum* spp.) and lavender (*Lavandula* spp.).

Mixed grass border frames waves of
sedums and flowers.

TURF THAT GRASS

*The day of the traditional "perfect" lawn and
suburban model of row upon row of manicured
domains is over. Using chemicals in the name
of turf is simply not sustainable or acceptable.
Revamping your lawn may mean ripping it out
altogether—or finding dramatically different ways
to use and care for it.*

1 **GO SMALL.** Consider increasing your garden and reducing your
lawn to the bare minimum size for a friendly game of bocce
ball, croquet or badminton.

2 **NARROW IT DOWN.** Treat it as pathways in between a series
of raised beds, vegetable plots or orchard rows. For a holistic
approach, you can use your organic grass clippings as mulch on
the adjoining gardens.

3 **PLANT IT UP.** Transform an existing patchy lawn full of
dandelions to a bee-friendly wildflower meadow by regularly
overseeding with wildflower mix. Plug in bulbs, too, and allow
them to naturalize.

LAWN AND ORDER

If you don't want to lose the lawn, embrace these earthwise eco tips to keep it strong yet sustainable.

1 TOSS ON SEED. Choose the grass seed most suitable for your conditions to overseed lawns or start new patches from scratch. To overseed means sprinkling new seed over existing turf. Do this each season and toss on lots, selecting lower- and slower-growing varieties for best results. Well-seeded turf has more staying power.

    TIP: If you have a large space that is not being utilized and has become overgrown with weeds, a lawn can actually work as a simple solution. Regular seeding and mowing will wipe out weeds and keep things tidy while you contemplate landscaping options.

2 MULCH AND MOW. Use a sharp mulching mower, which will leave clippings on the ground to naturally break down and add nutrients to the soil. Keeping the blade as high as possible will avoid scalping the surface and reduce weed-seed penetration and water demand. If you trim your lawn's edges regularly, this will reduce the time required to mow.

3 **RETHINK DEAD ZONES.** Take note of areas of lawn that look lackluster. Down the road, you may wish to create a new garden space out of a lifeless patch—why not consider a raised bed stuffed with edibles? Or, if the area is shy of sun, try pruning back surrounding shrubs or trees to let in more light.

4 **ADD NUTRIENTS.** Come spring, use slow-release-organic fertilizer and top-dress with sand, topsoil, compost and manure (or a combination). Add ¼ to ½ in. (½ to 1 cm) of top-dressing materials and lightly brush into the lawn with the backside of a rake. (The object is to get the material down to soil level.) Also, add lime seasonally, sprinkling a light, even layer over your lawn.

5 **WELCOME WEEDS.** Change your expectations from the perfect weed-free lawn to a safe family- and pet-friendly green space. Have you ever heard your dog or small child complaining about the odd dandelion or clump of clover?

6 **STAY DRY.** Let your lawn go brown during the summer drought—this will spare you from some mowing and save precious water. Once the rains start again, your grass will green up in a jiffy.

AERATE AND INVIGORATE

Aerating your lawn is a sustainable way to boost its health. Reducing soil compaction at the turf crowns improves drainage and enables fertilizer, oxygen and moisture to get to the grass. If you have a football field, you can rent a professional motorized aerator and run it across the entire lawn (just watch out for the little pellets of soil flying through the air). But for smaller spaces, here are some non-motorized options.

It is best to aerate during dry weather at least twice a year, in early spring and late fall. There's a bit of mystery surrounding the act of aeration, but in actual fact it is super simple and does not require any fancy stuff—simply choose from these easy strategies.

FORK IT. The best tool for aeration is the classic pitchfork. Simply pierce the lawn at regular intervals, using the pressure of your foot. Ideally, you want to sink the fork at least 2½–4 in. (6–10 cm) into the soil every 6–8 in. (15–20 cm). Move along your lawn in a regimented fashion as though mowing it, so you don't miss any spots. Switch your pitching foot from time to time to avoid fatigue.

SLICE AND DICE. For more dramatic aeration and soil conditioning, slice into your lawn at similar intervals with an edging tool.

TAKE A POWER WALK. Put on some golf shoes or cork boots and do some serious trekking across your turf. This won't be quite as effective as the other options, but will nevertheless let your lawn breathe a little easier.

Maiden grass, *Miscanthus sinensis* 'Gracillimus'

MASSES OF GRASSES

We're not talking lawn here, but rather a sweeping, flowing mass of ornamental grasses to frame your landscape in a luxurious, low-maintenance manner.

Consider the elegantly classic *Miscanthus* maiden or silver grass. Or plant up other gorgeous contenders like red baron (*Imperata cylindrica* 'Rubra'), Mexican feather (*Stipa tenuissima*), bronze leather leaf (*Carex buchananii*), blue oat (*Helictotrichon sempervirens*) and black mondo (*Ophiopogon planiscapus* 'Nigrescens'). These grasses are all very sexy and at home in the garden. Don't forget to plant them in masses and clumps. Choose several—they all work wonderfully side by side with many contrasting textures, colours and sizes.

Scottish broom, *Cytisus scoparius*

INVADER ALERT

Do you know everything that's growing on in your garden? As gardeners we need to guard against invasive weeds taking root in our outdoor areas.

Plant explorers have been bringing home non-indigenous seeds and plants for generations and even today all it takes is picking up a new plant to wind up with an unexpected guest. Some of these new introductions are outcompeting indigenous plants, spreading rampantly along roadways and ditches, hitching rides in vehicle tire treads, sticking to boat bottoms, hiding in pre-planted hanging baskets and elbowing their way into your yard at every opportunity.

The most invasive plants—such as Scotch broom, morning glory and blackberry—cause massive damage to native ecosystems, providing little or no advantages to wildlife, and creating fire and health hazards and erosion concerns. Compounding the problem is that noxious weeds have little likelihood of being controlled by deer or other grazers.

If you believe you have a noxious weed problem in your garden or backyard, take these steps.

1 **RESEARCH.** Thoroughly identify the plant in question so that you don't eradicate native plants by mistake. It is also in your best interest to ensure the weed will not threaten your safety. If you have giant hogweed, for example, proceed with caution—wear gloves and/or get expert advice as the sap contained in the hairs covering the plant and in the stems can cause skin rashes and burns.

2 **REMOVE.** Now that you know what you are dealing with, pull or dig up noxious weeds—and the earlier the better. Getting to the root of the problem as soon as possible will prevent these weeds from digging in so deeply that they become a nightmare.

3 **RAZE IT.** At the very least, cut off and continue to level new emerging growth. This regular practice will reduce the weed's ability to photosynthesize and its vigour will decline.

4 **REPRESS NEW GROWTH.** Roll out a temporary cover of heavy black plastic in the heat of summer to smother smaller plants and seeds. Open, disturbed spaces are magnets for invasive plants, so best to keep them covered until you can plant them up.

5 **REPLANT.** At the end of summer, replant with desirable choices, keeping an eye out for the undesirables. Or replant the open area with a temporary cover of turf. Lawns can usually out-compete noxious weeds, as the regular mowing stops these plants from gaining strength. Eventually, you can remove the turf and plant this area up, or keep it grassed and establish your new garden elsewhere. This may be best in areas where such invasives as Scotch broom have set foot and left multitudes of seeds that will lie dormant for decades—waiting for their chance to rise up once again.

FRIENDS AND FOES

How do you feel about deer, mice and rats in your garden? One may be prettier than the other two, but all can wreak havoc, as can rabbits, raccoons, moles and birds. Use these tips to keep your garden intact.

STEER AWAY DEER. Delightful as they may be to watch, these foragers can be destructive to gardens. The only certain method of control is a properly designed barrier. Effective fencing at least 6 ft. (1.8 m) high can be fashioned from bamboo, reed grass, plastic, mesh wire or rope, recycled skis, old bicycles, wooden pallets and more—the options are endless. Still, you don't need to fence yourself in entirely. You can contain particularly vulnerable gardens but leave the rest of your landscape open. For a variety of tricks to keep deer from devouring everything in sight, see "Deer Oh Deer", page 48, for our ideas on this!

REPEL RABBITS. When fencing for deer, choose a fence with a tight enough weave to also dissuade rabbits, another ravenous gobbler of edible plants. You can also purchase non-toxic rabbit repellents that will fool bunnies into thinking a predator lurks nearby.

FEND OFF RATS, MICE AND MOLES. Smaller rodents are some of the most troublesome and damaging pests. Ask for a natural mouse and rat repellent—a perimeter pest control that can protect your garden with the strong scent of spearmint and peppermint. Other over-the-counter deterrents use the scents of such predators as the fox and bobcat. Whatever you do, keep it sane and humane. Toxic bait is a frightening method that should be avoided at all costs— not only is it a horrible way for any animal to die, but it runs the risk of poisoning other creatures higher up the food chain, such as large birds, raccoons and, of course, foxes and bobcats. (And toxic bait is also a danger to children and domestic pets.) Live or kill traps for rodents are effective as long as you monitor them on a daily basis. Lastly, be sure to keep gardens clean and free of rotting fruit and improperly managed compost heaps and garbage. And encourage rodent predators such as owls and hawks to your garden by including perch trees and nesting areas.

BYE BYE BIRDIE? Birds are friend and foe to the gardener because they help control insect populations but also damage berries and other food crops. Enjoy the best of both worlds by welcoming feathered friends to some areas of the garden, while using visual and reflective deterrents to dissuade them from spots where vulnerable plants and crops reside. Hanging old CDs or recycled aluminum pie plates in trees and bushes works well. You can also place sentries that signal danger, such as a fake great horned owl made from holographic flashy materials.

CARE ABOUT BEARS. It's best for bears—known for their intelligence, adaptability and keen sense of smell—if we give them no cause to visit our garden. Do everything you can to keep a debris-free yard and healthy non-smelly compost bin. Store pet food indoors and keep garbage cans well sealed and inside a garage if possible. Pick fruit and berries promptly. Not only can a bear do a lot of damage to a garden and put humans at risk, its own survival is jeopardized when we lure it out of the wild and into our yards.

DEER OH DEER

Over time we've learned to celebrate both the trials and tribulations that come with living in tune with nature. And there are many ways to discourage deer without becoming completely cagey.

When dealing with deer or any perceived threat to the garden, we avoid aggressive fencing. An impenetrable compound is just too stifling. Certain areas of the gardens—such as the salad patch, a newly planted sapling or a hosta collection—may need to be protected this way, but certainly not an entire property. Who wants to live in a cage?

A better solution is to rethink your garden design. Only plants that are particularly vulnerable or worthy should be granted additional care and protection. Everything else can be left to fend on its own, with susceptible plants re-thought altogether or positioned behind daunting plants for deer (spiky or very dense shrubs, hedges and perennials).

Wondering where to start? Here are some tricks to allow you to live with the deer.

L–R: Purple allium, *Allium hollandicum*
'Purple Sensation'; sea holly, *Eryngium*
'Sapphire Blue'

USE BAD TASTE. Add only those plants less likely to be nibbled. While at times it may seem that simply everything is an option for hungry or curious deer, generally speaking, plants that are woody, hairy, spiky, fragrant, silver-coloured or indigenous are less likely to attract attention. See "Bambi-Tough Bulbs," page 62, for more ideas.

SPRAY IT ON. Use natural deer-repellent products to spritz on young trees until they grow high enough to be out of reach. Note: keep these liquids well away from hands and clothing as they are often very smelly. And avoid spraying them directly on the edible parts of plants. A liquid fence of non-toxic egg and garlic may also repel deer.

THINK BIG. Plant taller trees with branches starting above grazing height (about 5 ft./1.5 m), or use a temporary encirclement of fencing with stakes and/or wire fencing until they reach this height.

STAY OFF LIMITS. Vegetable patches should be properly barricaded but your fence doesn't have to appear prison-like. Plant edible and thorny climbers with berries along the fenceline to attract birds and bees. Espaliered fruit trees are a good choice to line the inside of the fence, while grape and kiwi can climb along the top rail. Birdhouses and bee boxes can endow the post tops to finish off your eco-fence.

HAVE A BLAST. Dogs and kids help to dissuade foragers with their oodles of energy and noise, but don't allow them to chase the deer. Planting your garden near a well-used pathway, door or road also provides protection through day-to-day action.

MAKE A MOTION. Moving objects also repel deer. Hang CDs, aluminum plates or tins, flagging tape, ribbon and fabric to blow in the breeze and help to deter hungry nibblers.

ADD SURPRISE. The shock of simple water sprayed from a sensor-activated sprinkler is highly effective. It's also a good way to cool off when weeding or gardening! At night, sensor lights also work to spook deer from your landscape.

GO UNDERFOOT. Ground surfaces can be chosen to deter deer. These include noisy gravel, sharp rock, pavers or less grip-able surfaces such as slippery wood decking, bridges and boardwalks.

GET COMPLICATED. Browsers such as deer are looking for an easy meal, so make it difficult. Forcing them to deal with drop-offs, ravines, retaining walls, hedges, stairs and water features such as ponds and creeks in order to access your garden will help to keep deer in check.

MOVE ON UP! Rooftop gardening is all the rage and is an ideal place to raise food crops and honeybees.

MATERIALS

Clean rags

Steel wool

Motor oil or WD-40 (or in a pinch, use a light cooking oil such as canola)

TOOL TIME

Here's an easy and worthwhile task for a rainy day: polish up your garden tools. Apart from getting major spousal brownie points for just a little effort, those neglected gardening tools slung in an outdoor corner will thank you, too.

1 First, collect your tools. Even if they are wet from being left out, that's okay.

2 Use a rag to wipe down all the metal parts, removing grunge and any organic debris. Remove rust with steel wool.

3 Next, take another clean rag and wipe down any plastic or wooden handles.

4 Dip the first rag into motor oil and wipe down the moving parts of your tools, including screws, rivets or hinges.

5 If you're really keen, protect wooden handles with a light application of tung oil or wood stain and protector.

6 Allow the tools to dry in a warm, moisture-free space, and store in a protected area.

Columbine, *Aquilegia vulgaris*

Opposite, clockwise from upper left:
Tea, *Camellia sinensis*; native trillium,
Trillium ovatum; creeping thyme, *Thymus
praecox* 'Purple Carpet'

GROWING GREENER

*Want to make your garden more eco-friendly?
Take these 10 easy steps towards backyard
sustainability and enjoy having less work as part
of the bargain!*

USE INDIGENOUS PLANTS. Often the best gardens are those that
resemble our wildlands. But it's more than using a few native plants
within a traditional ornamental garden setting. Fully native gardens
(forest- or meadow-like) are low maintenance and always look
good despite the occasional spell of neglect. You'll spend less time
mowing, watering, fertilizing and pruning.

GO WITH THE FLOW. When rain streams off hard surfaces such as
asphalt and concrete, the result is flooding and soil erosion. Instead,
use as many permeable surfaces as possible, such as specially
designed grass pavers or aggregates for driveways and sidewalks.

HOLD BACK THE HOSE. Water only when essential—which isn't often.
When you do, soak the ground to encourage healthy and deep root
development—this will reduce the future need for supplemental
irrigation.

RIGHT PLANT FOR THE RIGHT PLACE. By matching site conditions—such
as shade, sun, space, drainage and soil—to your plant selections, you
will reduce the need for unnecessary maintenance. Match perennials

Constant Warrior

The sword fern *Polystichum munitum* is a sharp contender for almost any planting situation. Deer-resistant and drought-hardy, it survives the harshest sun-baked site yet thrives in damp shade. Perfect in combination with a grouping of vines or Japanese maples, the sword fern works well in masses and the fronds will provide a gorgeous weed-suppressing groundcover. Maintenance is simple. To keep a neat and tidy appearance, cut old fronds back prior to the new spring growth emerging. This is truly a low-maintenance native plant that will grow in suburban backyards, urban courtyards and naturescape reclamations. We even grow them on the roof of our woodshed!

with early-spring bulbs so they cover up each other's spent foliage. Choose drought-tolerant trees to plant in large groves, or dig masses of hardy blowy grasses into difficult sites. Plant where space allows to avoid unnecessary shearing and heavy pruning later on.

CUT BACK ON CLIPPING. If you are not confident in your pruning cuts then simply don't snip. Overzealous pruning of plants and trees will create big problems and additional care and resources will be required to restore their health. When pruning, stick to the four Ds: dead, damaged, diseased and duds.

GO ORGANIC. Think long term and begin to build your soil. Organic-based fertilizers are definitely better for your garden's health and originate from the farm, forest, ocean (seaweed, fish) and land (minerals). The healthier the growing conditions, the better your plants will be able to ward off disease and pests, as well as deal with drought.

SCROUNGE UP MULCH. Continue to layer mulch on your garden bed every year. Having 2–4 in. (5–10 cm) of mulch over your garden is a great goal to strive for. It will reduce weeds and slowly decay, adding organic material that keeps your soil permeable and at moderate temperatures. After applying mulch, the introduction of beneficial insects such as ladybugs will help keep your garden healthy and beautiful.

MAKE A MEADOW. There is nothing prettier than a field of wildflowers with a curving path. A push mower will suffice for the minor amount of maintenance and you will attract a wide range of wildlife. Naturalizing bulbs also work well in fields, as do birdhouses and feeders. Let's replace all those manicured mowed lawns with beautiful meadows. Or, grow your own wheat or other grain such as spelt or oats instead of lawn and enjoy a small-scale harvest.

GROW A ROW. Build or buy a greenhouse to provide extra opportunities to grow food all year long. And add extra vegetable beds for friends and family. Tuck in herbs throughout your gardens and plant leeks, garlic and chives wherever you have space. They taste great, look amazing and attract pollinating bees and other beneficial insects.

GO NUTTY OVER EDIBLES. As you fill in spaces, or give away plants as gifts, always consider edibles. Nut trees, fruit trees, edible climbers such as kiwi and berry bushes and canes, plus novelty plants such as *Camillia sinensis* (tea), will help you and your neighbours grow greener.

GET GROWING

Once things start to get established in the garden, why not branch out a little? Think of your landscape as a long-term art project. Weed out issues and embrace your chosen plant palette—wildflowers, grasses, succulents, edibles, or what have you. Enjoy growing vegetables? Then you owe it to your inner gourmet to experience the wonders of a year-round food garden. Not hungry? Well, it's never too late to finally learn a few pruning tricks!

SPRING FLING

If you want to enjoy a beautiful spring flower-bulb display, you must plug bulbs and corms into the ground during fall. Sometimes it's not easy to get motivated to plant something with no promise of any immediate reward but it doesn't have to be difficult. And you'll appreciate the amazing spring surprise, starting with the first emerging leaves in late winter. Here's how to pack more punch into your bulb displays.

KEEP ADDING. Right after your fall garden cleanup, tuck a few bulbs in any empty spaces. Try some under tree canopies or within existing clumps of perennials, where bulbs can emerge through the supporting foliage. Over time, the routine habit of adding several clumps of bulbs each season will accumulate into a dramatic show.

CREATE CLUSTERS. The old style of planting single bulbs (all carefully placed "pointy" side up) in single holes can be sped up to create better bulb displays. Simply select a larger space in your garden, dig a shallow hole and tip your newly purchased bag of bulbs into it, spreading the bulbs throughout the space to create a single layer. While you're doing this, quickly arrange the bulbs to point upwards and then cover with soil. Grouped plantings like this will have more impact in your garden.

Nice Bulbs for Naturalizing

- Allium
- Anemone
- Camus
- Crocus
- Daffodil and jonquil
- Dog's-tooth violet
- Glory-of-the-snow
- Hyacinth
- Siberian squill
- Snowdrop
- Starflower
- Species tulip

L–R: Crocus, *Crocus vernus*; species tulips, *Tulipa* sp.

BUY IN BULK. Buy large packs of similar bulbs to create masses of uniform colour—or, conversely, look to lesser quantities of specialty bulbs to create splashes of dramatic interest. Bulbs that will naturalize and reproduce, such as snowdrops and narcissus, are a wise choice, as you will never have to dig them up to divide and replant. Simply get them into the ground and look forward to years of enjoyment.

THINK DEEP. A good rule of thumb is to plant bulbs to a depth of two times their length in milder environments. Consequently, smaller types like anemone, species tulips and crocus will be planted fairly close to the surface, while the large daffodils and hybrid tulips need to be planted deeper. In cold climates, gardeners should plant their bulbs even deeper (three times their length) for added protection from frost.

BONE UP. An application of bone meal is beneficial when planting bulbs, but is not required after the initial planting. Be careful to avoid inhalation when applying dusty products such as bone meal, and place it at the bottom of the hole where it will benefit root production.

IT'S NEVER TOO LATE. If you wait too long or forget to plant spring bulbs, don't despair. You do have another option. In springtime, nurseries offer flowering bulbs in containers, ready to be instantly transplanted into your spring garden.

L–R: Chocolate lily, *Fritillaria lanceolata*; crocus, *Crocus vernus*

Opposite, L–R: Blue drumstick allium, *Allium caeruleum*; hyacinth, *Hyacinthus orientalis*

BAMBI-TOUGH BULBS

For those lucky enough to live in areas visited by wildlife, being careful to plant only critter-resistant bulbs will save your garden from becoming spring salad for a herd of deer. If you're unsure, plant bulbs in moderation at first and spread the risk around your garden. Selecting multiple varieties of bulbs will also help, no matter what you choose. While there are no guarantees, particularly when food gets scarce, here are the best bets for bulbs resistant to squirrels, gophers and deer:

1 **ALLIUM.** These beautiful globe-like members of the ornamental onion family repel deer with their pungent odour. They naturalize easily and make excellent cut and dried flowers. Try *Allium aflatunense* 'Purple Sensation', *A. atropurpureum*, *A. caeruleum* syn. *azureum* and *A. giganteum*. A more unusual pick is *A. moly* (golden garlic or lily leek), with spheres of cheerful yellow flowers blooming on strong leafless stems.

2 **BABOON FLOWER (*BABIANA STRICTA*).** Grown from a corm, the fragrant star-shaped blossoms of this beauty attract butterflies but seem to deter peskier critters.

3 PINEAPPLE LILY (*EUCOMIS BICOLOUR*). With its attractive foliage and striking flowers, the pineapple lily is a showstopper (though you'll have to watch for snails, which like to nibble the leaves).

4 FRITILLARIA. Try sensational *Fritillaria imperialis* for drought-tolerant clusters of nodding flowers, great for borders and butterflies.

5 SNOWDROPS (*GALANTHUS NIVALIS*). Often the first blooms of the season, these delightful and dainty white blossoms naturalize well.

6 HYACINTH. Most fragrant hyacinths do well in deer country, including the foolproof *Hyacinthus orientalis* 'Double Hollyhock' and 'Purple Sensation'. The smaller *Muscari* or grape hyacinth is another naturalizing deer-proof pick, as is *Scilla campanulata* 'Excelsior' or wood hyacinth. Triplet lily (*Brodiaea laxa*) 'Queen Fabiola' is a wild hyacinth, great for around trees and shrubs.

7 NARCISSUS. Despite their cheerfully bold colour, daffodils are distasteful to deer. Try *Narcissus cyclamineus* 'February Gold' and *N. jonquilla* 'sundial', double-flowering *N.* 'Cheerfulness' and *N. jonquilla* 'Bell Song', along with *N.* 'Chromacolor', *N.* 'Cassata' and *N.* 'Dutch Master'.

Wildflower mixes often include California poppy, *Eschscholzia californica*; shasta daisy, *Leucanthemum × superbum* and field poppy, *Papaver rhoeas*

Opposite: Wildflower meadow including elegant clarkia, *Clarkia unguiculata*; field poppy, *Papaver rhoeas*; California poppy, *Eschscholzia californica*; cornflower, *Centaurea cyanus*

WATER-WISE WILDFLOWERS

Drought-tolerant wildflower beds and meadows can be easily established in an empty garden bed or over sections of your existing lawn.

MATERIALS

Wildflower seed mix

Black plastic (if you are replacing lawn)

Eco-fibre, compost, manure and landfill green waste

Flowers That Work Well in a Wildflower Garden

- Black-eyed Susan
- California poppy
- Coneflower
- Dame's rocket
- Iceland poppy
- Prairie aster
- Shasta daisy
- Shirley poppy
- Yellow lupine

TIP: The annuals such as California poppy will flower early on, offering colour until perennial plants such as Shasta daisy are established.

1 To plant up an existing section of lawn with wildflowers, cover the desired area with black plastic to kill the turf grass, which can then be easily removed using a spade. During hot weather, this process will take about a week. Once the grass is dead and lifted, you can compost this material in a pile if you wish.

2 Dig up your new flowerbed and add plenty of organic fibre (eco-fibre, sustainably sourced peat moss, compost, manure and landfill green waste are all helpful).

3 Once your bed is ready, seed generously with a wildflower seed mix comprised of an equal blend of native grass, annual, perennial and biennial flowers. Look for a blend designed for your geographic area, such as West Coast wildflower mix.

4 Including grasses in the mix will physically support the younger flowers, as well as help deter unwanted weeds. To create a natural meadow effect you can also make up your own seed mix. Simply blend equal amounts of sheep fescue grass seed (or use other attractive, non-aggressive bunching grasses such as blue oat and blue fescue) with your favourite wildflower seed.

5 After planting, irrigate on allowed days. Once the garden is established, you should not need to water.

6 Adding clumps of spring bulbs each year will help to extend the flowering season. As the grasses and summer-flowering plants mature, they will hide any spent bulb flowers and leaves.

7 For a strong show of blossoms, overseed with fresh wildflower seeds each year. Sprinkle over disturbed soil, in the spring and winter, after removing unwanted weeds.

MATERIALS

Sticks or stones

Penknife

Permanent marker

KNOW YOUR ROWS

There are many seed-row markers available at your local nurseries but here are three ways to easily whip up your own for a pretty and practical addition to your garden.

1 Collect large Popsicle sticks or purchase them from a craft store. Use a marker to note your seed type and place the stick at the head of your row to mark its place.

2 Cut twigs to size and use a penknife to scrape away some bark. Once you have a flat surface on the side of the stick, write on it and plug it in.

3 Or, scour the beach for flat-faced stones. Write them up and position in your planting bed.

SWEET SUCCULENTS

Given the current interest in water-wise plants, succulents—from Sempervivum *to* Jovibarba *to* Echeveria—*are hot. Their brilliant red and green cushions and spiky rosettes are striking wherever they grow, from containers to rock gardens to drought-hardy beds.*

CONTAIN THEM. Most often, succulents are used for container plantings or tucked into the crevices of landscape rocks. Have a look around your garden and you'll probably find lots of sunny nooks and crannies to tuck in a succulent or two. A stone wall is a perfect perch, replicating our natural rocky slopes.

HANG THEM. Rework a traditional hanging basket or create a living wreath or sculpture to hang or use as a table centrepiece. Or keep it simple and plant succulents along the edges of retaining walls for a blast of colour and flowers in summer and beautiful robust foliage the rest of the year.

CARVE A BOWL. Decaying tree roots and beach stumps may be hollowed out to create crevices to hold succulents. Succulents prolifically propagate, so once you invest in a few plants you'll have plenty of material to work with before you know it.

FILL A HOLE. For those who are tight on space, succulents don't ask for much. Miniature gardens can be crafted by taking a large piece of pumice or landscape rock and carving or drilling small crevices and holes to fill with succulent plantings.

Take these measures to ensure your succulents survive the winter:

USE A BLANKET SOLUTION. *Sempervivum* (houseleek or hen and chicks) and *Sedum* (stonecrop) are both quite tolerant of frost and moisture. For the most part, you can leave these in the garden. Protect hardy in-ground succulents during a cold snap by covering your crop with a blanket (burlap works well), but always remove it before any rain.

PROTECT POTS. Regardless of frost tolerance, all container-planted succulents will need to be protected. Bring pots indoors and treat your succulents as houseplants through the late fall and winter. Or, store potted succulents in a well-ventilated hothouse or insulated cold frame.

METER MOISTURE. Really succulent or "juicy" plants such as *Echeveria* can barely tolerate frost. In extreme cold the fluid in the leaves may expand, causing frostbite and irreparable damage. The combination of hard frosts and pounding rain can turn these beautiful rosettes into blackened mounds of mush. *Echeveria* is best planted in movable containers that can be carted inside during the season.

TAKE ROOT. As an extra precaution, place some plants into dormancy so you will have a fresh supply come spring. Simply collect succulent rosettes and remove the soil from the roots. Place in a shallow tray filled with pebbles and put in a dark, cool place. Spritz the plants once in a while to keep them moist.

SET THEM IN THE SUNSHINE. Mass planting of succulents is easy, as they quickly spread to fill in any gaps after initial planting. Although there are very few spots where succulents won't look great, most don't thrive in full shade, although they will persist for several years. They'll thrive best in rocky or sandy soils and don't require fertilizer or supplemental irrigation once established.

BED REST

By late fall, the summer vegetable garden is a riot of tangles, colours and seed pods. It's time to cut a path through the chaos and put the garden to bed for the winter. And, while you are doing this, to make the most of a last lovely harvest.

SAVE SEEDS. Peas and beans are among the easiest seeds to save for next year. We leave a good quarter of our peas and beans on the vine for this purpose. By late fall, the pods are husky and crumbly. Pick them on a warm day to ensure as little moisture as possible remains in the pod. If the pods are damp, lay them on a mesh screen and dry indoors. Once shelled, the peas should be slightly wrinkled and the beans smooth, dry and often multi-coloured. Discard any rotten or disfigured seeds, and place the rest in paper envelopes in a cool, dry place. Remember to label the envelopes with the year and cultivar and any helpful tips you've learned from growing them.

TAKE STOCK. Even if you didn't have time to plan or plant a winter veggie garden, don't dismay. Take a look at what's left of your summer vegetables to see if anything can make it through the next season. For example, if it hasn't already gone to seed, Swiss chard can be cut back and will rise up again to provide greens throughout the fall and winter. Plus, keep your kale, cabbage and Brussels sprouts right where they are to enjoy harvesting these frost-resistant veggies throughout fall and winter.

TIP: Cut off any blossoms to extend your harvest of winter greens.

STORE ROOT VEGGIES. Late carrots, potatoes and beets may be kept in the ground and harvested as needed, but the risk of rot is high during the wet seasons. It's a toss-up as to whether it is better to pick root veggies and store them in a dark, cool place or risk leaving them in the ground. We do both.

GATHER HERBS. Herbs such as rosemary, thyme, parsley and sage may stay green enough to use throughout a mild fall and winter, especially if you cut any flowers back and mulch with straw or leaves to help protect the plants from frost. To be extra safe, pot up a small amount of these herbs and other faves to bring indoors to a sunny windowsill.

TIDY UP. Once you've sorted through your vegetables and decided what can linger through winter, it's time to start cutting back and cleaning up the refuse. Trellises and nets should be taken down on a dry day and stored for next year. Plant matter can be chopped up with a shovel and sent to the compost heap. By now, the mulch that protected your veggies through the summer has likely broken down enough to be turned into the soil. A fork works well for this task.

GIVE BACK. Amending your soil by adding rich organic material is a way to give back some of the nutrients used up by your summer harvest. Compost, well-rotted manure and rinsed seaweed are a few local amendments readily available. Depending on the needs of your soil and the richness of the amendments, 4–6 in. (10–15 cm) of material over your garden bed is usually about right. Dig the mixture right into the soil by using a fork or shovel.

BLANKET YOUR BEDS. Another 3–4 in. (8–10 cm) of leaves, preferably minced (simply run them over with a lawnmower prior to raking), should be spread over the top of the bed to protect the soil, keep the heat in and deflect any weeds. By early springtime, this leaf mulch will be rotted enough to mix into the garden and you'll be ready to plant.

MULCH BERRIES. If you have a strawberry bed, weed it out now and allow the plants to harden off and experience a frost or two before mulching heavily with pine needles or straw for the winter.

TIP: Pine-needle mulch is best saved for acid-loving plants like strawberries or blueberries.

WINTER GREENS

MATERIALS

Driftwood, untreated mill off-cuts or rough-cut cedar

Cardboard or newspaper

Garden soil and/or compost mix

Summer-started seedlings for transplanting

Willow saplings, beach sticks or PVC piping

Medium-weight clear plastic

Clamps

Coroplast

Cloches (optional)

Why not start a garden in summer for winter harvest? Extending the vegetable season does more than fill your pantry—it lets you try your hand at different plants that thrive in cooler weather or need the nip of frost to taste their best. The rewards of growing during this time of year are abundant—you'll have fun, save money and enjoy fresher, more nutritious vegetables than you'll find in local stores. It's easy, too, with fewer pest and watering worries than a summer-harvested patch.

1 Due to weather extremes, site selection is very important to successfully extend your season. Start by tracking the sun throughout spring, summer and early fall to see how the seasonal movement will determine exposure. Choose the warmest, most sheltered spot in your garden. In a perfect world it will be positioned on an open, south-facing slope. A large landscape rock can also attract and trap heat for plants. Remember that sandy, loamy soil will retain heat better than dense clay soil. If your soil is on the heavy side, add organic matter, compost or rotted manure.

2 In early fall, make a raised-bed "container" by fashioning and securing a rectangle of lumber to fit your designated garden space. You can use driftwood and mill off-cuts or rough-cut cedar. Select from materials on hand and always avoid pressure-treated lumber when growing food.

3 Line the bottom of your bed with cardboard or newspapers to smother weeds and lawn underneath.

4 Fill your bed with high-quality garden or compost soil mix. An alternative is to layer scrounged manure, seaweed, coffee grounds, lawn clippings, peat moss, sawdust and/or chips from untreated wood, compost, sand and leaves with a top base (4–6 in./10–15 cm) of soil.

5 Now plant up your bed, leaving generous spacing between plants to allow lots of light and discourage slugs from moving in for a winter slumber. If you're well prepared, you'll have summer-planted pots of broccoli, kale, leek, cauliflower, cabbage, horseradish, Jerusalem artichoke, kohlrabi, parsnip, rutabaga and turnip ready to plant up. Frost will not harm these crops, but will actually sweeten and improve their flavour. You can also add lettuce, arugula, chard, carrots, beets, parsley, spinach and cilantro with a little extra care and protection from rain, snow and frost. If you didn't start your plants in time for this, don't despair. Many nurseries stock vegetable bedding plants for fall and winter gardening.

6 Now create a cover; essentially you will be building a mini-greenhouse over your bed. An easy row cover can be fashioned from a cut sheet of Coroplast, a flexible product that lets light through. Bend it into a semi-circle shape and secure with 8-in. (20-cm) wooden posts or rebar, or score it lightly with a knife and fold to create a free-standing cover. Don't forget to cut pieces to cover the ends, too.

Another simple row cover uses flexible PVC pipe as bracing. You'll need six 5-ft. (1.5-m) lengths of 1-in. (2.5-cm) PVC pipe, twelve 1-ft. (30-cm) lengths of rebar and a roll of medium-weight polyethylene. Push one pair of rebar pieces 6 in. (15 cm) into the ground 2 ft. (60 cm) across the row. Press opposite ends of a length of the PVC pipe firmly in place over the top of the rebar, forming an arc. Repeat with each length of PVC pipe, spacing the arcs 18 in. (45 cm) apart. Unroll the poly film and extend it lengthwise, over the arcs along the entire length

of your row. If it is not wide enough to cover the entire arc, you will need to overlap two lengths of poly film to form a complete cover. Secure the plastic to the pipe with clips, staples or heavy-duty tape. Place rocks along the outside lower edges of the plastic to prevent it from flapping and tearing. Be sure to leave enough plastic at either end to close the row cover at night or during cold weather.

You can also protect single plants or seedlings with a cloche or any cover that encourages sunlight to warm the soil beneath. Traditionally made of bell-shaped glass, cloches ease a maturing veggie through winter harvest, or protect tender seedlings. Fashion cloches from various treasures from your recycling bin—large deli jars or semi-transparent plastic milk or juice jugs (topped with a rock to hold them steady in the wind) work very well.

Cold frames are more permanent structures, topped with clear plastic, glass or fibreglass to collect heat from the sun's rays. Cold frames may be stationary or portable, depending on your needs and choice of materials. Choose a south or southeast location for your cold frame with good drainage and adequate shelter. A wall or hedge that provides protection from winter winds in the north is ideal. See "Clever Cold Frame", page 78, for building advice.

7 Regardless of your cover of choice, ventilation for cold frames, row covers and cloches is critical to maintain a healthy environment for your plants. Raise the top during the heat of the day and close it up again early enough in the afternoon to keep the heat in overnight. To protect your crops further during colder weather, insulate at night by covering your cold frame and cloches with burlap sacks or old blankets.

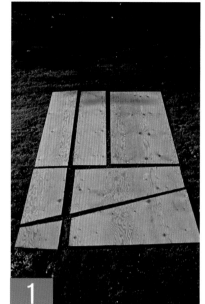

MATERIALS

Tools:

Wood clamps

Circular saw or handsaw

Drill

Carpenter's square

Screwdriver

Hardware:

#6 × ¾-inch round-head
galvanized screws

#8 × 1½-inch flat-head
galvanized screws

Four door hinges, 4-inch
galvanized with screws

Two ¼-inch plexiglas acrylic glazing,
37⅝ inch × 30⅜ inch

Eight corner braces, 3-inch

Optional: two 3-inch bolts and nuts

Plywood:

One sheet 4 × 8-feet exterior grade
¼-inch plywood cut to fit (see diagram):

Front: 5 × 1 foot (152 × 30.5 cm)

Back: 5 × 2 foot (152 × 61 cm)

Two sides: 1 × 3 × 2 foot cut
to shape shown

CLEVER COLD FRAME

A minimalist cold frame can be constructed with just one single sheet of exterior-grade plywood if you measure and cut carefully. You'll finish with a back, front, two ends and a shelf. Measuring 5 ft. (1.5 m) wide by 3 ft. (91 cm) deep and 2 ft. (60 cm) high, this portable frame can shelter a sizeable crop of cold-season veggies from winter's winds. Once you assemble your materials, you'll need six to eight hours for this project—we know it's more complicated that our usual "simple," but it's so worth the effort because with it growing food becomes a snap!

Lumber:

Cut the following rough lengths from 2 × 2-inch lumber to use as inside frames:

Front frames 60 inch (one bottom); 60 inch (one bevel to fit against top edge); plus 10 inch (two)

Back frames 60 inch (one bottom); 60 inch (one bevel to fit top); plus 20 inch (two)

Side frames 32 inch (two) and 34 inch (two) cut to fit

Lid frames 34¾ inch (four); 30⅜ inch (four)

Handles (optional) 6 inch (two)

Shelf (optional)

One 10 inch × 5 foot ¼-inch plywood notched to fit

Four 8-inch 2 × 2-inch scraps to use as shelf ledge

Lid props (optional)

Two 1 × 2 inch × 4 foot

For Base:

Paving stones or bricks (30 linear feet)

1 Sketch an outline and cut the plywood using the dimensions provided. Note that two scrap pieces will also be produced. Cut the 2 × 2-inch lumber into framing pieces, using the approximate dimensions provided as a guide.

2 Begin with the back piece and attach the corresponding 2 × 2-inch pieces to frame the interior edges of the back panel. Drill and screw in place using flat-head screws (pre-drill holes to avoid splitting 2 × 2-inch lumber). Repeat the same procedure on the front piece using the corresponding 2 × 2-inch pieces. Attach the 2 × 2-inch pieces to the top and bottom interior edges of each side panel, plus handles (optional) leaving room at each end to allow it to fit against the front and back interior framing. Attach each side first to the back panel (corner to corner) and then to front panel. For extra strength use exterior carpenter's glue prior to screwing into place.

3 To make lids, attach corresponding 2 × 2-inch pieces to form two equal rectangles (37⅝ × 30⅜ inch). Reinforce inside corners with corner brackets. Attach plexiglas by drilling and securing to top of lid frame with round-head screws. Fit lids to top of cold frame and attach two hinges to each lid and against the back outside edge.

4 Create a prop for your lids by attaching two 1 × 2 inch × 4 foot pieces to the front of your cold frame with a bolt and nut. Positioning a screw (top extended ¼ in.) on the outside bottom edge of the lid (centred) and drilling holes in 10-inch increments along the rod allows you to fasten the rod to the frame when it is elevated and prevent a crash should the rod shift.

5 Attach the shelf piece by notching the corners and securing it to a ledge created by screwing small pieces of scrap 2 × 2 inch to the inside back and sides. The shelf will create valuable space in your cold frame and it's handy for trays of seedlings.

6 As an option, paint the inside of your assembled cold frame white to reflect the sunlight onto plants. The finished cold frame will be portable and should be set on blocks of concrete or bricks to protect the bottom from rot.

L–R: Leek in bloom, *Allium ampeloprasum* var. *porrum*; garlic, *Allium sativum* ; Harvesting garlic, leeks and chives.

Opposite: Chive, *Allium schoenoprasum*

TOUGH-LOVE TRIO

Plant a trio of tough culinary alliums: garlic, leek and chive. Individually, each has a loyal following, but combined in the garden this pungent trio is unbeatable for fabulous food, beautiful blooms, great border foliage, disease resistance and pest control. Even better, all allium blooms attract birds and butterflies and make beautiful cut flowers.

FALL FOR GARLIC. First up, garlic (*Allium sativum*) is an important culinary herb with uses in many Mediterranean dishes, along with contemporary, modern cuisine. It also has strong medicinal qualities and is an immune strengthener. In the garden, garlic is architecturally strong with impressive slender stalks and twisting "scapes" that can be snipped, steamed and eaten as a garlicky green. It keeps pests at bay and works wonderfully tucked in between larger shrubs or planted as a narrow row between a bushier border of chives and thick-stalked leeks.

Purchase seed garlic, or simply obtain some locally grown organic garlic in spring or fall to plant in a sunny location where it is not too moist. Garlic loves sandy soil, but can grow pretty well in a variety of conditions. It's a heavy feeder and appreciates a hearty dose of organic fertilizer right after planting to jumpstart and sustain the bulb (so we often throw a small handful of complete organic fertilizer right in the hole, when planting). Garlic is grown from cloves pulled from the head, skin on. Plant them individually about 1 clove deep and spaced 4 in. (10 cm) in rows 18 in. (45 cm) apart. Each clove will produce a single bulb to be harvested in late July to early August. Plant garlic between a row of chives and leeks for a culinary allium display.

GO GLOBAL. Leeks (*Allium porrum*) are another wonderful culinary allium, cultivated for more than 3,000 years. The stalks and bulb are disease resistant, tasty and nutritious, but did you know the blooms are also absolutely bold and extravagant? Along with chives and garlic, leeks make a surprising stand-in for ornamental flowering alliums. Simply plant leeks in rows and commit to leaving every second one to bloom at the end of the season. Like their ornamental cousins, any of the trio of culinary alliums will provide show-stopping, globe-like blooms, at a fraction of the cost. We call it the lazy gourmet way.

Leeks are best started from seed and transplanted to the garden when the seedlings are the size of a small pencil. Separate the seedlings and plant very deeply, about 4 in. (10 cm) beneath the soil to encourage deep, white stalks near the roots. Space leeks about 6–8 in. (15–20 cm) in rows at least 1 ft. (30 cm) apart.

CUT AND TASTE. Chives (*Allium schoenoprasum*) grow easily and lushly and make a wonderful low border to accentuate the taller forms of alliums like garlic and leeks. Snip them and enjoy in abundance! With a light onion-like flavour, chives are spectacular in salads, omelettes and just about everything. In late spring and summer, small orbs of purple chive blooms will attract bees to the garden and the buds may also be enjoyed as simple cut flowers or edible garnishes.

Chives are best planted from division, readily available by splitting large clumps with a shovel or edging tool. Simply dig them up and slice into smaller clumps. Remove the top green growth with scissors and replant each clump in the garden 4–5 in. (10–13 cm) apart in a row to create a thick border.

Boxwood, *Buxus sempervirens*

HEDGE FUN

Thinking about planting a hedge? The options are almost endless and you needn't default to a common cedar subdivision hedge unless you want to. Cedar hedges have their place, but there are many other materials available for creative gardeners.

RIGHT PLANT, RIGHT PLACE. A hedge is very useful for providing privacy from neighbours and for calming traffic and other street noises. They can also benefit wildlife by creating much-needed nesting habitat and food. As is always the case, choose the most appropriate plant for your desired result and pay careful attention to site conditions. And, wherever possible, select plants that will thrive under occasional pruning.

GROW A HEDGEROW. You can do something radical and mix up your choices, perhaps staggering beech trees, hawthorns, hedge maples and yews. Very common throughout Europe, hedgerows provide year-round beauty and are less prone to diseases than hedges that consist of a single plant type. Plus, a hedgerow offers a less fussy shape than a formal hedge, making it easier to look after. It will also provide welcome bird habitat for nesting.

GO TO THE BEECH. Beech-tree hedges are a classic. Even though they are deciduous, beech will usually hang on to its dried greenery, providing interesting leafy texture and visuals in winter, along with tranquil rustling sounds when windy.

EAT IT UP. How about an edible hedge? New varieties of columnar or espalier apples can easily be trained into a living border that will offer up spring buds and a bounty of fruit.

LOVE YEW. Evergreen, glossy and classic, the yew tree is tidy, drought tolerant and easy to keep clipped. However, deer tend to nibble on it.

EXPLORE THE POSSIBILITIES. Other hedging alternatives to consider include purple-leaf barberry, spotted laurel, evergreen huckleberry, blueberry, boxwood, Russian olive, holly, hemlock, native cedar, lilac, escallonia, berberis, osmanthus, bay, arbutus, Mexican orange, willow, California lilac, skyrocket juniper and cypress.

Opposite: *Buxus sempervirens* (boxwood)

JUST CLIP IT

If you're a novice at clipping, hedge your bets with easy-care English laurel and boxwood. A fast-growing habit allows both to bounce back from misplaced cuts in a single season. Nevertheless, learning to prune them properly is a good investment in your yard's ongoing appeal. Aim to prune twice—once in early spring and again in late fall before and after birds have nested—for best results.

KNOW YOUR GOAL. To prune a laurel or boxwood, first decide on the height. You can dramatically shorten or narrow either of these hedgings without loss of health or appearance. Next, select the most suitable tools depending on how much you plan to snip. Loppers and pruning shears (hand or motorized) are all that are required to maintain shrubs up to 4 ft. (120 cm) tall. For higher hedges, you may require an orchard ladder. And if it's been more than a couple years between clippings, you might want to pull out the chainsaw to slice through larger branches.

TAKE IT SLOW. Begin cutting the hedge back to your selected height. Stop and step back often to check progress and straightness. Go easy at first, as you can always take more off later. Once the desired height has been achieved, begin straightening the sides of the hedge with your pruning shears. Again, peruse your work often as you go.

CLEAN UP CUTTINGS. Next, remove loose branches and leaves from the ground and from within the hedge. While your hedge may look a little bald at first, have no fear—within a month or so it will have grown new leaves and will look lush again.

Storm Warning

Leggy and uneven growth invites damage during storms. Do some proactive pruning on your shrubs and trees to keep them healthy and compact. When winter storms arrive and swaying trees frazzle the nerves of homeowners, many people rush to cut large trees to prevent them from doing damage to homes or falling across power lines. But before you prune or top a tree, consider the outcome carefully or you may do more harm than good. Consult an expert arborist if you are unsure.

4-D PRUNING

When pruning, start with the four Ds—branches and limbs that are dead, damaged, diseased or duds. Only after you take care of the basics should you try to fine-tune your trees and shrubs.

1. **DEAD.** Every season, watch for inevitable dead limbs and branches on your trees and shrubs and remove them. If you're unsure of whether or not a stem is dead, scratch the surface bark with a sharp knife or the edge of your secateurs. If the inside is green, the branch is still alive but if the underside is dried and brown, it is likely dead.

2. **DAMAGED.** Next, remove any limbs or branches that are badly torn or bent. Make a clean cut adjacent to the next node, bud or branch for best results.

3. **DISEASED.** Remove diseased stems as quickly as possible to prevent the malady from spreading to other areas of your tree or shrub.

4. **DUDS.** Feeling confident now? Lastly, remove any poorly pruned stubs, suckers or waterspouts, then step back to admire your perfectly pruned plant.

Consider Before You Cut

WHEN TO PRUNE?

Many evergreen shrubs and trees can be clipped year round, but the low-stress seasons of spring, fall and winter are usually best. For routine pruning, pay attention to blooming habits. Trees and shrubs that bloom in summer and early fall should be pruned in winter or early spring. Spring bloomers should be pruned right after their blooms begin to fade. Pruning ornamental flowering trees and shrubs right after flowering may net you a bonus of a second flush of blooms in plants such as lavender. But don't use this technique on fruiting trees and shrubs or you will cut off the fruiting buds. Prune these plants when they are dormant—usually in late winter and early spring, well before they are scheduled to bud out.

TOP CONCERN

Refrain from heading, topping or shearing trees. This only creates ugly and unnatural-looking stems, while increasing the chance of disease. Topping a tree triggers the same reaction as pinching back does in annuals—encouraging thicker, denser growth at the stub and numerous weak side shoots. In the wind, this new growth can act like a sail, making the tree more likely to fall. Rather than topping trees to create stubby plants out of tall forms, consider opening up and thinning them instead. Another problem is the lollipop syndrome, when gardeners shape flowering trees and shrubs into balls and compromise future growth.

SHEAR HERE

Shearing (making multiple overall cuts of new growth for shape, rather than selective pruning cuts) does work well for grasses and hedging materials such as boxwoods, along with lavender and heathers (shear after blooming). You can also effectively shear shrub roses.

UGLY RECOVERY

Have you ever done a brutal pruning job on a tree or shrub? At best, be prepared to kick yourself as you gaze at the misshapen structure. At worst, poorly pruned trees can be unsafe, as the underlying trunk may be compromised by misguided cuts.

FORGET A QUICK FIX. If you need to repair pruning mistakes, have patience. Your once-pretty tree or shrub needs time to recover and there is no snap-your-fingers solution. Simply stop the pattern of poor pruning and allow the plant to begin the process of regrowth while you nudge it along.

CONSIDER A COMPLETE OVERHAUL. When the severity of plant pruning is major, the only really effective method for recovery is what's called renewal pruning. This involves removing all stems to encourage new growth from the ground up. Renewal pruning works wonders on blueberry, red twig dogwood and many flowering shrubs, and is a very effective way of correcting years of neglect. Timing-wise, very early spring is usually best. This technique will even work for trees that are slowly declining and in need of renewal, such as arbutus. Usually the woodier the plant material, the less inclined it will be to respond to this technique of severe pruning.

TAKE STOCK. Fixing poorly pruned trees is a more challenging process. First, identify what went wrong, stem-by-stem, and evaluate whether further removal is necessary. For trees and shrubs to fully recover from bad cuts, great patience and sometimes compromise is required. Often the best approach is to celebrate the unique shapes created by mistakes. As long as you are mindful of removing any potentially weak and hazardous limbs or branches, you can consider the mangled tree or shrub a unique living sculpture.

WEED OUT PROBLEMS

During spring and fall, it's amazing how fast a new crop of weeds can be generated by a few dew-filled mornings. Luckily these same wet conditions also make their removal easier. While dry, sun-baked soil is difficult to cultivate, damp soil encourages weeds to pop out. The bottom line: pull them promptly before they go to seed.

1 **HANDS DOWN.** The most effective method of removing weeds during cool, wet weather is to manually pull them by hand.

2 **CHOOSE YOUR SPOT.** If weeds are overwhelming you, simply grab a bucket and visually slice off a section of your garden patch to start with. This shouldn't take more than a few minutes and you can congratulate yourself on completing your goal. Every bit helps, and every weed you yank before it goes to seed will save work down the road.

3 **DO NOT DISTURB.** If you have allowed weed seeds to set and broadcast, be careful not to stir up your garden more than necessary—loosened soil will invite a fresh crop of unwanted plants.

4 **SUN BAKE.** While pulling weeds is more difficult in the hot months, there is an advantage. During the dry season, you can use a hoe to uproot weeds, then simply allow the heat of the sun to shrivel them up. If you've caught them before seed has set, toss into the compost bin.

5 **SPRAY VINEGAR.** A simple way to get rid of unwanted weeds and grass in the cracks of driveways, patios and walks is to apply vinegar (household or concentrated). Always spritz vinegar-based herbicides on a hot day, as the heat assists in the process. Multiple applications are sometimes necessary for vigorous contenders such as horsetail.

FAST FERTILIZER FACTS

We know we should feed our gardens, but with so many choices of fertilizers, it's easy to be stumped about where to start.

UNDERSTAND THE GROUND RULES. Fertilizer mostly comes down to four basic types: powdered, granular, time released and liquid. Powdered fertilizer provides fast access to nutrients. Pellet or granular fertilizer is easy to spread. Time-released pellets have a coating that allows the nutrients to diffuse slowly through an outer shell. And liquid fertilizers are sold as a concentrate that needs to be diluted with water—sprayed or sprinkled, it is quickly absorbed throughout the entire plant.

KNOW THE NUMBERS. All fertilizers will display their percentages of nitrogen (N), phosphorus (P) and potassium (K). For example, a 100-lb. bag of 10-3-3 will contain 10 lbs. of nitrogen, 3 lbs. of phosphorus and 3 lbs. potassium. Nitrogen stimulates leaf and stem growth, phosphorus promotes healthy root growth and supports seed and fruit development, and potassium is important for fruit and berry quality and enables cell division to occur in roots and buds, which is essential for vigorous growth. What else is in the bag? Organic materials (and/or fillers) and other micro-nutrients.

GO NATURAL. Earth-friendly plant foods are available from a range of sources and offer a balanced approach to nutrients that helps to stimulate the growth of beneficial micro-organisms in the soil. Animal manures from cattle, sheep, chicken, horse and even alpaca supply a slow and steady flow of nutrients. Blood meal is high in nitrogen, while bone meal supplies phosphorus. Dried fish waste and fish emulsions are well-rounded and supply all three elements. Less common but very effective suppliers of phosphorus and potassium are rock phosphate and green sand. Limestone is a very important supplier of calcium and will help balance soil pH levels. When you are considering fertilizer, think long term and build up your soil by using enriching organic fertilizers, rather than a quick-fix chemical fertilizer. The healthier your growing conditions are, the better your plants will be able to ward off disease, pests and drought.

ADD MULCH. Collect and scrounge as much organic mulch as possible, such as chipped tree waste, bark mulch, straw, dried lawn clippings, leaves and seed-free weeds to add to your fertilization efforts. Layer it on your garden bed every year. As it slowly decays, the organic material will keep soil temperatures moderated while allowing moisture to permeate.

TAKE TIME FOR TEA. If you want an awesome homemade fertilizer, try brewing up some compost or manure tea. Simply place a small burlap bag of manure or compost in a large pail of water and let sit overnight. Strain into another bucket or barrel and use a watering can to apply to your garden weekly.

Comb the Beach

For those who live near the sea, a rich concoction of seaweed and fallen leaves is found treasure for your garden. When spring rains swell, fallen leaves travelling in sea-bound creeks are snagged by clumps of beach-stranded seaweed. The combination of nutrient-rich seaweed and carbon-loaded leaves is a dynamic duo for your garden beds. Collect this material well above high tide to ensure you are not endangering sea life. Some folks insist on rinsing the salty sea residue from seaweed prior to adding to the garden. Frankly, we don't bother.

L–R: Snake bark maple, *Acer pensylvanicum* 'Erythrocladum'; silver birch, *Betula pendula*

Opposite, clockwise from upper left: Pink prickly heath, *Pernettya mucronata*; spring heather, *Erica carnea* 'Springwood Pink'; Christmas rose, *Helleborus* sp.; heathers, *Calluna vulgaris*

A BLAST OF BOLD

In winter, well-chosen plantings add interest to your landscape and stand out from the otherwise monochromatic green background. Consider these gorgeous cool-weather additions and enjoy unexpected colour, textured bark, seed pods and winter "fruit."

1 **TAP THE POWER OF THE BARK SIDE.** Burning bush (*Euonymus alatus*) is a hot pick with searing fall colour and cork-like bark. Redtwig dogwood (*Cornus sericea*) and new cultivars of willow (*Salix*) such as 'Flame' offer a stunning show of red, yellow and orange stems after leaves have dropped. Himalayan (*Betula utilis*) and Chinese birch (*Betula albosinensis*) are ghostlike and gorgeous with white trunks and branches, while arbutus (*Arbutus menziesii*) and strawberry trees (*Arbutus unedo*) offer up a deeply textured, masterpiece of richly toned peeling bark. Paperbark maple (*Acer griseum*) is equally distinctive with bright cinnamon-toned bark that shreds off in thin papery flakes, while snake bark maples (such as *Acer pensylvanicum*) has a vibrant striped skin of various colours.

L–R: Rosehip, *Rosa rugosa*; witch hazel, *Hamamelis × intermedia* 'Jelena'; white prickly heath, *Pernettya mucronata* 'Alba'.

Opposite: Corkscrew hazelnut, *Corylus avellana* 'Contorta'

2 **FLOAT ON WAVES OF FLOWERING FOLIAGE.** Flowering heathers (*Calluna vulgaris*) provide stunning waves of foliage and flowers when we need them the most, while the handsome Helleborus or Christmas rose is an incredible gift to the winter garden.

3 **GET HIP.** Many roses (*Rosa*) are prized for their plump hips, glowing ruby red on the darkest of days. Edible, they can also be picked and simmered into a jelly jammed with vitamin C.

4 **BEWITCH BY BLOOM.** Witch hazel (*Hamamelis virginiana*) glows like a beacon in winter with fragrant yellow, orange or red flowers. Cornelian cherry (*Cornus mas*) will also flower early, with yellow flowers standing out along bare stems.

5 **BE SEEDY.** Prickly heath (*Gaultheria mucronata* 'Alba'), Japanese snowbell (*Styrax japonicus*), silver bell (*Halesia tetraptera*), goldenrain tree (*Koelreuteria paniculata*) and the dove tree (*Davidia involucrata*) are lush with seed capsules that dangle like ornaments from bare branches.

6 **TWIST AND SHOUT.** Coveted by holiday flower arrangers, corkscrew willow (*Salix matsudana* 'Tortuosa'), black locust (*Robinia pseudoacacia*) and hazelnut (*Corylus avellana*) stand out with their curious curly branches.

NO RULES

Get serious about gardening by breaking a few rules. Nature changes things up all the time, resulting in stronger varieties of plants and more diversity. You might be surprised to learn that pushing the envelope when it comes to garden design and maintenance often results in a more balanced, ecological and economical overall outcome. Who says you have to buy plants when you can grow your own, for example? Look around and question the status quo. Remember, there's the right way, the wrong way and the gardener's way.

PLANT MATH

If you want to create more pizzazz, not to mention more plants, just apply some basic math: add, subtract, divide and multiply!

ADD. If you can't afford to buy large plants but want instant impact, don't be afraid to double up. Plant two small lilacs, lavenders or roses together and amplify your effect. Over time, you won't notice the separate shrubs, unless the blooms happen to be different colours (which can offer exotic allure).

SUBTRACT. Some plants, like succulents, regularly produce offspring. Keep parent plants healthy and increase your stock by routinely subtracting the babies and potting them up.

DIVIDE. When purchasing garden stock at nurseries, look for plants that are bursting out of their pots. Perennials particularly, like Oriental poppy and chives, love to be divided. In the spring, use a fork or spade to pull or slice the clump into two, then plant up both.

MULTIPLY. Sedums may be started in trays by simply pulling parent plants apart and potting up pieces of individual stems. Just a few small sedums create dozens of new ones that will root quickly and be ready to plant out in six weeks or so.

MATERIALS

Any tired woody shrub

Large pot (optional)

Potting soil

Pruners

JUST STOOLING

Woody shrubs such as lavender or heather have a tendency to fail after three to five years, becoming weak and sparse. If your woody shrubs are less than robust you can propagate some fresh recruits by the stooling method.

1 Remove the weak shrub from the garden and trim damaged, diseased or dead stems.

2 Place your shrub in an empty pot, ensuring there will be enough space to bury the entire plant from root to tip. Alternatively, you can bury the shrub in a garden, creating a stooling mound.

3 Add potting soil and cover the entire plant, leaving just 4–6 of the uppermost tips (2–3 in./5–8 cm in length) exposed.

4 Press the soil firmly around the tips and water well.

5 After several weeks, the tips will form roots of their own and may be treated like seedlings. Push back the soil and release the new plants from the parent stem. Gently pull or snip your new "stooling" with pruners.

6 Your baby shrubs may be potted up or planted directly into the garden.

LAYERING IT DOWN

Most people think of seeds and cuttings when they make reference to plant propagation techniques. However, these are not a gardener's only choices when it comes to making more plants. Another method is layering (air layering, simple layering and French layering). Whereas cuttings are associated with small snippets, layering techniques can be practised with mature growth and often result in larger plants sooner.

UP IN THE AIR. Air layering is done on large established branches, in the air, without uprooting the plant. It is often used for tropical plants, especially if they have become gangly and need to be shortened, or if several plants are desired. Choose a stem and twist or lightly scrape the bark with a pocketknife in several places at the point where you wish to have roots develop. Pack pre-moistened potting soil around this area by wrapping it with a garbage bag. Tie the bottom tight and then insert one or two straws in the top before tying it tight on top. These will allow you to add water during the rooting process. In time, roots will develop, filling the rooting medium and allowing you to cut the stem below this area to release the new plant.

DOWN ON THE GROUND. Simple layering is most often utilized under a large rhododendron or woody herb such as sage. Scrape the bark or twist as before, except this time simply insert the low-lying branch under the soil's surface or lay compost or mulch over top. If the branch is further above the surface, place the branch in a bucket, pot or any container filled with a good growing medium mixed with sand, or a compost and mulch mix. Be sure to keep the branch from moving by placing a brick or other heavy object on top or by pinning it down with a bent piece of wire looped over top. The growing medium should remain moist, with as few fluctuations as possible in conditions. After a season of growth, new roots will develop and the branch can then be cut off and replanted elsewhere.

GO FOR MORE. French layering takes these steps further and allows for increased production. Make multiple scrapes along the length of a branch, covering each with soil and pinning them down or stabilizing them with small weights. After roots appear, each piece may be cut and replanted.

MATERIALS

Woody shrub such as
lavender or rosemary

Willow juice (see sidebar)

Small containers

Potting soil

Scissors or secateurs

FREE PLANTS

*Stem cutting is a form of propagation best
used for woody plants and shrubs such as
rosemary (*Rosmarinus officinalis*) and lavender
(*Lavendula*). If you have a bit of patience, it's a
good form of propagation to play with and allows
you to make new plants quite successfully from
existing shrubs. To make new plants you'll need
to collect some cuttings—there are a number of
methods for doing this, however you'll have great
results with this simple and super-easy technique.*

1 Use clean secateurs to snip several stems (about 3-4 in./7–10 cm long) from the woody plant. Strip and remove the leaves from the bottom portion of the stem. Dip this end into powdered rooting hormone or willow juice (see sidebar).

2 Next, plant the stem in a small container or nursery flat, filled with a half-and-half mixture of sterilized potting mix and sand, planting the "dipped" end of the stem down into the soil.

3 Place your pot or flat in a warm spot, such as a heated cold frame or greenhouse, or bring inside to a windowsill. Water it well. After several weeks, roots will begin to emerge at the bottom of the stem and a new plant will have formed. After several weeks, you can transplant your rooted plant to a new container.

Making Willow Juice

Native willow (*Salix*) contains properties that encourage root formation and aid propagation. You can dip your cuttings in willow juice and expect similar results to using rooting hormone. To make willow juice, simply collect a bunch of willow stems with leaves intact. Cut them into small pieces and place in a heat-proof container. Add boiling water to cover. Allow to cool and strain. Dip your cuttings in the juice and plant them up.

COOL IDEAS FOR HOT COMPOST

Did you know that your backyard compost can be used to propagate and grow heat-loving plants? These techniques may be traced to gardeners of yesteryear who often looked for simple and thrifty ways to increase their garden productivity.

1 HEAT THINGS UP. Propagate new plants using the warmth of your working compost pile. Simply place trays of potted-up cuttings or seeds on top of the compost to enhance germination and encourage a vigorous root system. Cover the trays with a transparent plastic lid to speed things up even further. This method of germination and propagation is reminiscent of placing seedling trays on the warm top of a refrigerator or over horticultural heat cables.

2 GET GROWING! When seasonal temperatures slow food production, use your compost pile to mimic the warmer soil temperatures of spring. First, stir the pile with a fork to mix up the ingredients. Level off the top and place pots of growing medium or a layer of sandy soil directly onto it. Growing crops like carrots, squash and potatoes this way will extend your growing season. A simple glass or transparent plastic cover early in the season will enhance your compost garden with a greenhouse-like effect.

L–R: Lupin, *Lupinus* sp.; sunflower, *Helianthus annuus*, in field of poppy, *Papaver somniferum*

Opposite, L–R: Wisteria, *Wisteria sinensis*; feverfew,*Chrysanthemum parthenium*, poking up from bay leaf, *Laurus nobilis*

CHEERS FOR VOLUNTEERS

Volunteers are plants that just pop up, either by self seeding or reproducing via tap roots and natural layering processes. Some may be weeds but others are worth celebrating. And if volunteers show up where you don't wish them, simply dig them out and replant.

1 **FLOWER POWER.** Prolifically self-seeding poppies and calendula pop up readily. While lupines, bachelor buttons, feverfew, Japanese anemone, hollyhock, lady's mantle, columbine, foxglove and mullein may appear to flower season after season, it is actually new volunteer plants growing alongside the old that have rapidly matured and provided that second and third show.

2 **GO WILD.** To encourage volunteer plants, toss a handful of wildflower seed around and allow the new plants to naturalize in and around your garden.

3 **BUSH OUT.** Larger woody plants like lavender, heather and Japanese maples will also voluntarily sprout from seeds. Many succulents such as *Sempervivum* will create genetically identical babies called offsets, which may be pinched and planted.

4 **SHOW TOPPER.** That new plant that made a surprising showing is not impossible. Bird droppings or the bottom of your boots can bring in amazing new seeds.

5 **NEW ROOT.** Seeds are not the only source of volunteers. While pruning, bits of plant material that fall into the garden or are dropped enroute to the compost heap can root and become exact duplicates of the original you were trimming. Similarly, you can purposely pop cuttings into the ground to encourage volunteers.

6 **ROCK BOTTOM.** To find volunteer plants, scrutinize the bottom of slopes or rock walls, or any spot that might capture rolling, falling or blowing seeds.

7 **LAYER IT ON.** Layered plants (ones that root themselves when underlying branches are covered with soil) are another treasure worth looking for, especially fast-growing climbers like wisteria.

8 **SEE YOU, SUCKER!** Suckering shrubs and trees—think sumac, angelica and shrub roses—may also be dug up and newly appreciated.

SUMMER LOVING

Sometimes, there's just not enough love going on in the garden. If you think you're having a pollination problem in your vegetable garden and are not willing to leave it solely to Mother Nature, you can simply take matters into your own hands.

What causes lack of pollination? Perhaps it is the well-documented challenges that our honeybees are currently facing. Or other times it can be due to changes in seasonal weather patterns.

How do you know if pollination isn't occurring? A telltale sign is a tree or vegetable with lots of flowers but little actual fruit that "sets." This happens with berries, tomatoes, fruit trees and particularly with squash. Here's how to take control and push pollination along.

MAKE LIKE A BEE. If you have a male zucchini or squash flower, or can ask a neighbour for one, you can pollinate the female blossoms yourself. Using a Q-tip, simply insert the end into one open flower, pick up some pollen and then move on and place it on the next flower.

AVOID CONFUSION. If you're planning to save seed for next year, be careful to not mix one type of squash flower with another, unless you want to end up with a monster case of cross-pollination and a weird-looking "pumpkini"!

FIND FRUITFUL POSSIBILITIES. Tomatoes may also be pollinated; fruit trees, too. For smaller flowers, a toothpick works best. Be gentle to avoid damaging the delicate blossoms.

On chair: Butternut, *Curcurbita moschata*; kabocha, *Kabocha nimono*; and acorn, *Curcurbita pepo* winter squashes. Heirloom lemon cucumber, *Cucumis sativus* 'Lemon'

Seed Surprise

When saving seeds this way, you may occasionally get a surprise: a plant that is the result of previous cross-pollination with another, resulting in a mixed, or hybrid version of the original.

SEED SHOPPING

Here's a fun trick. Shop for seeds and food at the same time! If you want to try a funky new squash variety, or a tasty heirloom tomato in the garden, pick up the actual veggie, prep and enjoy it on the table, then save the seeds to grow in your own garden next year.

JUST DO THE MATH. A small organic Kabocha squash costs three dollars at our neighbour's farm stand. We can pick this up to eat for supper, then save the seeds for next season (and we'll have plenty to share). A seed packet alone costs about the same but is not nearly as satisfying. Locally grown, open-pollinated vegetables work best for this. Lemon cucumber anyone? It's a fun, frugal and dare we say *delicious* way to shop for seeds.

SIMPLY WASH AND DRY. Once you remove the seeds from your chosen vegetable, rinse off any residue and lay them out on a piece of newspaper or paper towel to dry. A few days later, once they are completely dry, store them in a paper envelope or recycled container and save for planting season.

PREPARE TO PLANT. If you're not sure about planting directions, simply look up your chosen vegetables in a seed catalogue and follow the directions given.

MARVELOUS MICROGREENS

You don't need fancy contraptions to grow your own delicious salad microgreens indoors. Simply sprout them on a windowsill or shelf with a basic grow light. Microgreens from arugula, broccoli, sunflower or pea seeds are easiest to grow—and all are wonderful in a sandwich or atop a salad.

1 Simply sprinkle the seeds very thickly on top of a shallow planting tray holding 1–2 in. (2.5–5 cm) of sterilized potting soil. Sprinkle a very thin layer (less than ⅛ in.) of soil on top and keep the whole thing moist.

2 Place the tray about a foot (30 cm) under an industrial work light fitted with daylight fluorescent bulbs (around $50 at a hardware store; or find it secondhand), or on a sunny windowsill.

3 Greens are ready to snip and savour in about two to three weeks.

MATERIALS

Untreated seeds

Shallow planting tray

Industrial work light with daylight fluorescent bulbs

Sterilized potting soil

A TRIAL BED

A trial bed is useful for gardeners to test how an individual plant will perform in a particular environment. It's always a good idea to test a new plant for a year before buying a bunch.

For example, not convinced of the enduring value of new trendy cultivars of purple coneflower (*Echinacea*), we tested a few in our garden. None survived beyond two seasons. This is a reminder to be wary of new "improved" cultivars that may be market driven and relatively unproved. Original species and long-established varieties are frequently the best bets.

On the plus side, an early blueberry test patch was doing so well we added many more plants over several years. These bushes are now providing enormous quantities of tasty berries.

A FAIR TRIAL. When beginning a trial in your garden, be sure to start with healthy plants and always factor in an establishment phase. All plants need to be pampered a little before they can show their stuff.

CHOOSE A NEUTRAL ZONE. Create a specific trial bed in an average zone of your garden not dominated by overpowering sun or deep shade. If your plant is not thriving, play around with different soil amendments and water regimes or move it to a different space to see if it prospers there.

NEIGHBOURHOOD WATCH. Another way to trial or audit plants without using up your own garden space is to identify and locate a plant you are curious about within a nearby public garden, park or even a neighbour's yard. Watch what it does over a couple of seasons without worrying about making the big commitment yourself.

TAKE AN AUDIT

Over the summer, we'd all benefit from putting aside our wheelbarrows, rakes and hoses for a few hours to perform a simple garden audit. An audit notes which plants are performing well, which ones are not, and other high and low spots. Collecting these thoughts while the evidence is all around us makes it easier to plan alterations to improve the garden in seasons to come.

CONSIDER THE BIG PICTURE. Grab a camera and take several overall shots of your garden. A panoramic lens will give you the widest view. Or simply stand in one spot and rotate your body and camera to obtain a collection of shots that can later be taped or "stitched" together electronically to allow a 360-degree look at your landscape.

NOTE DETAILS. Next, take some closeups of key plants and sections of your garden. Be sure to include weak areas, as well as potential spots for new gardens or landscape features.

JOURNAL IT. Print out your photos (or sort them digitally) and organize them into a print or online scrapbook.

TAKE NOTE. Jot down detailed comments next to each photo about plants, beds and features: What's working well? Looking healthy? Suffering? What do you need more of and what needs replacing? Walk around the garden to jog your memory as you do this.

SEEK INSPIRATION. Take a printed version of your audit into a nursery when you are seeking specific advice about plants or your landscape. And use your journal to record plants and design ideas from shops and other gardens as future fodder for your own outdoor space.

SMOOTH MOVE

When you have to sell your home or relocate, your beloved garden may be hard to leave behind. And who says you can't take it with you?

1 **SPEAK UP.** If you wish to take some of your beloved trees and perennials with you when you sell your home, be sure to note all the plants you want on the agreement for sale. Otherwise, buyers have every right to assume that what's in the garden comes with the house. Similarly, renters who have created or tended a garden on a landlord's property should discuss the movement of plants when giving notice.

2 **CONTAIN THINGS.** Start cuttings and transplants in pots well before moving, too—it is usually assumed that a container garden will move with you. For those in-ground perennials, trees and shrubs you have permission to take, pot up during cool weather if possible to avoid stressing the plants.

3 **WRAP THINGS UP.** Otherwise, lift the plants early or late in the day, just before the move, wrapping the rootballs in moistened burlap covered with plastic. Five-gallon buckets with handles are handy for moving small trees and shrubs. Smaller plants and bulbs may be wrapped in moistened newspaper and placed in boxes. If the boxes are covered, be sure to cut out large holes for air circulation. Keep everything moist, cool and out of the wind. Plan to pot or plant up your transports within a few days or at most a week.

4 **PROTECT AND PLANT UP.** Once you arrive at your new locale, place your specimens in a shady spot. Water well and get them in the ground as soon as possible.

MATERIALS

Shovel or spade

Tarp or wheelbarrow

TRANSPLANT TRICK

Do you have a large tree that needs to be moved? Is it too big to be heaved out of the soil? Well, don't bust your back! There is an easier way to get it up and out—simply use this backfilling technique to rock it right out of the ground.

1   Using a shovel or spade, begin by removing the soil around the tree, cutting and digging out a circle.

2   As the soil loosens, carefully lean the tree to one side a little bit at a time. Each time you do this, undercut the soil beneath the tree's rootball, removing as much as you can. Gently rock the tree to the opposite side and then fill the hole up again, using extra soil to really pack the cavity you just created.

3   Repeat as needed. Each time you rock the tree to one side and then the other, digging and backfilling, it will lift slightly.

4   Eventually the tree will be sitting at ground-surface height. Then you can simply pull the rootball onto a tarp for dragging into place, or roll it onto a wheelbarrow.

121

GOOD FUNGUS AMONG US

Have you ever wondered how natural forests and wild landscapes grow as well as they do? There's no fussing, rototilling or added fertilizer, yet they remain healthy and strong. This success is largely the result of a yearly influx of leaf litter and the natural presence of mycorrhizal fungi and beneficial bacteria.

When gardeners mimic the natural forest and apply a regular application of mulch, they are helping to improve their own garden soils with good fungus too. Fungi is present in undisturbed soil, however, rototilling, fertilizing, pesticides and allowing bare soils to compact deplete this natural population.

Gardeners have traditionally concentrated on feeding soil with an application of nitrogen, phosphorus and potassium (NPK) alone. A belief that soil is an inert root-holding medium ignores a complex biological myriad of fungi, bacteria and earthworms. Yet, it's easy to add fungi to your garden to boost this complex root support system. You can purchase mycorrhizal fungi and beneficial bacteria at your local garden nursery. Simply mix a handful into your planting holes

before adding seedlings, shrubs and trees. Or sprinkle fungi on top of existing gardens around plants and trees. For best results, provide a protective layer of mulch or compost over it. For the little bit of effort, the benefits are big!

MUTUAL DIVIDENDS. Mycorrhizal fungi connect with a plant's root system to form a symbiotic relationship that enhances the plant's nutrient intake, health and growth. Soil texture is also improved, and the hardworking fungi also couples up with nitrogen-fixing and phosphorus-dissolving bacteria, strengthening roots.

LESS FERTILIZER. With the addition of fungi, a reduced amount of fertilizer is needed—and should only be slow release and organic based—along with plenty of compost.

MORE VITALITY. Plant tolerance for stress will increase along with the ability to block the uptake of salts, encouraging healthy plant growth in poor urban soils. Fruit-bearing plants will be able to support heavier crops and bear at an earlier age.

IMPROVED DROUGHT TOLERANCE. Irrigation requirements will be lessened, especially if fungi are added in combination with a healthy cap of organic mulch.

PEST ARREST

Gardens are ripe for the wrath of several pests including slugs, snails, wireworms, cabbage worm, root maggots and the carrot rust fly. Chemical pesticides have been a quick fix in the past, but they are simply too dangerous and no longer acceptable. Just think of the consequences. Do you want your children or pets playing in puddles of poison? Do you want to crunch into a carrot coated in chemicals? Use these non-toxic pest ploys instead.

LOOK AT THE BIG PICTURE. The key to pest control in an organic garden is balance. Ensure you are using the best possible soil, proper light, adequate water and lots of diversity in plant life. Mix up your plants and rotate them around from season to season to keep pests guessing. Leave space between plants to allow good air circulation. And apply plenty of mulch throughout the year—the layers of organic material will replenish the soil, creating a natural, sustainable balance.

COVER UP. Moveable permeable row covers work well early in the season for several crops, particularly carrots, which are susceptible to the root-destroying carrot rust fly maggot. Securely enveloping your garden will keep adults from laying eggs in your patch. If you already have the carrot rust fly in your garden, destroy all infected crops, plant any new carrots well away from the infestation, and eliminate Queen Anne's lace, a host weed belonging to the same family. Yearly crop rotation is also key, but do not interchange with carrot-family members such as parsley, celery, dill and fennel.

BRING IN THE GROUND FORCES. Adding beneficial nematodes (tiny microscopic organisms that exist naturally) to your soil and/or lawn will deter a variety of pests including European lawn chafers, cutworms, maggots, weevils and also flea larvae. You can buy nematodes at nurseries; simply mix with water and add to your soil when planting or before mulching, or sprinkle them on the lawn.

DO SOME DUSTING. Natural insecticides made from fossilized deposits of marine plants and algae, known as diatomaceous earth, are safe to use in the garden and effective against snails, slugs, ants, and pill and sow bugs. Keep in mind, though, that other insects (some beneficial) may also be susceptible.

LAY SOME BAIT. Pesky wireworms are easily lured to pieces of potato or carrots. Bury thin slices under the soil 6 in. (15 cm) away from newly planted seedlings or seed-potato rows. After a few days, simply pull up the potato slices, now full of worms, and discard (but do not compost or you will simply spread the infestation into your garden).

SNARE SLUGS AND SNAILS. Set simple traps such as laying a board on the ground for slugs and snails to slither under, or placing a folded newspaper beneath a potted plant. Check below these lures in the early morning and discard the pests. Also, nighttime inspection and collection with a flashlight will usually net a good haul of slimy critters. Eco slug baits containing iron-phosphate are highly effective. Traditional chemical slug bait, however, should be avoided at all costs, as it is extremely high in toxic nerve poisons that can harm people, pets and wildlife. Slug guards and copper barrier tape may work as safe deterrents in some environments, but we've found them less successful than these other methods in ours.

Keep It Clean

Ensure that dandelions and any wild weeds you collect for consumption have not been sprayed with chemicals—and always wash well before eating.

WEED EATING

Native to Europe and Asia, the dandelion (Taraxacum officinale) *is distained in most gardens as a noxious weed. Much effort and tons of toxic chemicals are dispensed each year in the flurry to defeat the dandelion. But why try to beat them when you can eat them?*

Herbalists recommend organically grown dandelion for its tonic effect on the liver and gallbladder, and as an effective blood-cleanser and curative for skin conditions. And there are several delicious ways to devour dandelion.

SIP IT. The leaves can be simply tossed into the teapot for a healthful green brew. Steep in hot water, strain and enjoy.

SERVE IT. Salad lovers can enjoy the youngest, most tender leaves of the dandelion in early spring, tossed together with chicory, lettuce and other greens including chickweed, another healthful edible weed.

ROAST IT. When roasted, the roots of the dandelion make an excellent caffeine-free coffee substitute similar to chicory. Gather at least 20 mature dandelion roots and wash and dry them well. Roast on a cookie sheet in a 300F (150C) oven for about an hour, until they turn coffee-coloured. Store in airtight jars and grind fresh to brew as you would coffee.

Stonecrop, *Sedum spathulifolium*; sea blush, *Plectritis congesta*; blue-eyed Mary, *Collinsia grandiflora*

Opposite: Mixed sedums and fescue grasses mingle on a modern rooftop.

GARDENS IN THE SKY

From the Hanging Gardens of Babylon to today's modern green roof, here's why sky-high growth makes good sense.

ECOLOGICAL. Green roofs are an effort to replace the planting space lost to the footprint of a building. As an added bonus, they reduce heating and cooling requirements and have a dramatically positive effect on the local temperature within a building. They also add to roof lifespans, are exceptionally attractive and offer recreation space. Green roofs also provide a sanctuary for birds and butterflies, reduce noise pollution, add fire prevention, manage storm runoff and filter pollutants out of the air and rainwater. Aesthetically they connect open spaces and provide urban green-way corridors.

EASY. It's important to note that a green roof must be designed and engineered specifically for growing. Modern green roofs are virtually self-sustaining and should only require a titch of care, perhaps a once-yearly weeding. Want a green roof at home? It's getting easier to do. Pre-grown, instant and interlocking green roof "flats" will soon be as common as metal, asphalt or cedar shakes. These modular sections can be moved about, allowing for repairs or new skylights or chimneys. And if a portion needs

replacing, you can simply yank it out and snap in a substitute. The new systems use very shallow growing mediums (made from volcanic pumice, organic matter and recycled clay bricks) to allow homeowners to install them with a bare minimum of load-bearing structural updates.

ATTRACTIVE. Natural meadow-like designs adapted to the roof environment can host dramatic mass plantings. Plant selections must also be rugged and suitable for the harsh conditions up on top. Chive (*Allium schoenoprasum*), succulents like *Sedum*, pinks (*Dianthus*), sea thrift (*Armeria maritima*), thyme (*Thymus*), grape hyacinth (*Muscari*) and fescue (*Festuca*) offer tried and proven green-roof cover. But plant selections are not only limited to low-growing specimens—with proper planning, large trees can also dress up a roofline.

QUAINT CONTAINERS

Up the cool factor on your containers and add a little green space to grow herbs, flowers or vegetables.

RECYCLE, RECYCLE, RECYCLE. Look around for large tin cans and olive-oil vessels, and even large household items such as rusting clawfoot bathtubs, chimney pots or old sinks. Almost anything with a depression and drainage can be potted up. Or, if needed, drill a few drainage holes—for example, an old rowboat makes an awesome raised bed.

SALVAGE STUFF! Wobbly wooden chairs, vintage leather suitcases and wooden crates make whimsical containers along garden paths. Suitcases may simply be opened up and put in place, adding soil, plants and garden statuary—think mushrooms and gnomes! In a forest setting, the idea is to make your vintage container look as if it has been there forever. Mosses, ferns and a few stones will look right at home.

GO AU NATURAL. Old stumps and driftwood can be hollowed out to house sedums or native plants such as huckleberries or blueberries, trilliums, ferns and mosses.

MAKE IT EDIBLE. Cherry tomatoes, herbs, lettuces, strawberries and edible flowers make a delightful and useful arrangement for a kitchen patio or entranceway.

AIM FOR THE UNUSUAL. A vintage typewriter as a mossy garden sculpture? Just line the cavities with fabric cloth, chicken wire and soil and plant it up. Easy as A-B-C.

MATERIALS

Steel wool

Protective paint or anti-rust finish

Wax or varnish

A LITTLE RUSTY

Love it or leave it, you can't escape rust outdoors, especially in moister climates.

Rust is simply surface oxidization of metal, a natural corrosion that occurs when it is unprotected and exposed to wet weather. Cast-iron outdoor furniture and antique garden accessories are most susceptible. Many of us love this natural patina and call it character. The warm red tones and mottled texture of rusty metal lend a homey look and feel to metal accessories. But rust will damage the integrity of metal surfaces and structures, and eventually they will deteriorate. Ultimately, you'll have to decide whether celebrating the rusty look is worth it. If not, protecting iron from excess rust is as easy as 1-2-3.

1 Use steel wool to remove rusty spots, if any, before applying the paint or finish.

2 Apply protective paint or anti-rust finishes every few seasons or so.

3 An object you love can be left rusty but protected too to slow down the decay. Apply a coating of wax or varnish right over the rust to resist corrosion and add years of life to your treasure while still retaining a rustic look.

TIC TAC TOE

Sometimes we're in the mood for an instant garden pick me up. Enter a collection of recycled terra-cotta drain tiles and a few pots of Irish and Scotch moss. One of the tiles, which John dragged home from a dump pile, happened to be one foot square, a perfect dimension for four-inch pots. What luck!

1 Position your terra-cotta drain tile where it can be admired. Line it with fabric cloth to create a bottom and fill it with potting soil.

2 Remove the mossy blocks from their pots and fit into a neat checkerboard pattern and plant them up.

3 Anything square, like a wooden box, would work as a planter. And if you don't have two different kinds of moss, you can also fill alternating empty squares with soil and top with pebbles.

MATERIALS

One-foot-square terra-cotta drain tile

Fabric cloth or burlap cut to fit inside

Five 4-in. (10-cm) pots of Irish moss

Four 4-in. (10-cm) pots of Scotch moss

TUNE-UP TIPS

Save time, expense and your strength with these sensible and strategic garden tips—work smarter, not harder.

1 **DON'T BREAK YOUR BACK.** Use a tarp or scrap piece of plywood with a handle to move large plants and shrubs in and around the garden. It's often easier to transport material low to the ground than to try and lift it up into a wheelbarrow. If a wheelbarrow is required, tip it onto its side before loading. Slide or twist the plant or object into the bucket and then carefully pull the wheelbarrow back into the upright position.

2 **ENROLL THE BUCKET BRIGADE.** Collect empty five-gallon buckets. You'll often find them behind restaurants. Your loppers, clippers and gloves will fit nicely into the bucket. A recycled bucket also makes a great weed container, easy to manoeuvre through beds and light enough to carry when full. Unless they originally held detergent or other chemicals you can even pierce holes in the bottoms and pot them up with tomatoes and other edibles.

3 **BACKFILL BONANZA.** Don't waste time digging and planting into the soil or new garden bed if you can backfill the area instead. A large plant can often be left on the surface, while you raise the bed with surrounding soil, bringing it up to a proper level. It's far easier than digging a huge hole and allows you opportunity to add plenty of loose, fibrous mulch around your new plants.

4 JUST RELAX. Create a handy spot to sit. When gardening, having a place to take a break is vital and you can't beat one that follows you around while you work. The newer plastic wheelbarrows make great seats when tipped onto their handles. Grab a beverage and a (gardening) book and slip into the curved crevice.

5 SMOTHER IT. Plan to reuse your cardboard or newspaper as a weed barrier when creating new beds or before applying mulch. Eventually it will rot, but not before helping to stifle any emerging weeds. If you decide to alter a garden bed later, you won't be frustrated by having to remove artificial weed barriers such as landscape cloth.

6 GET HOSED. A regular garden hose is a handy tool when laying out new garden beds. Use it like a string and outline the edge of your beds before you dig them up. The perfect design often takes numerous tries and the hose will allow for easy adjustments. If possible, choose a warm spring day, as a rubber hose will bend easier. Once you have experimented with a hose, try landscape-marking spray paint for speed and better flow.

7 HUNT FOR TREASURE. Look for hidden garden gems, overgrown or tucked away behind a large tree or shed. So often we don't realize that we have wonderful plants right in front of us, just waiting to be rediscovered, tidied up or moved into a new location

8 MULCH, MULCH, MULCH. Save toil and money by using mulch instead of soil to make up the bulk of your garden beds. Soil, compost or organic amendments can then be confined to the hole or space immediately surrounding your plants.

9 CONSIDER, THEN CUT. Pull back wayward branches before pruning to see how the remaining plant will look afterwards. Get a friend to help you, and step back and consider the cut. By bending branches into new positions, you may decide you want to save them after all.

10 BREAK FREE. Don't feel you have to throw away those broken-handled garden tools. Often the most useful tools are those that have sawed-off handles. Short-handled "scratchers" are our favourite tools for weeding and planting. And short shovels and rakes make working in the close confines of mature gardens much easier, plus they are perfectly sized for children.

DESIGN WISE

When it comes to garden design, make like a bog and soak up ideas from near and far. We love to travel for landscape inspiration—who doesn't?—but more often than not, we find the coolest ideas in books and magazines and in our own community. After all, there's no better way to see what will grow and work well in your garden than by snooping at a neighbour's place and the local park or public garden. And be sure to design a few key elements—a playhouse, gazebo or a well-placed bench—from which to admire your own private paradise.

Wit and Whimsy

A garden can make a formal statement or be a more casual ramble. But just like any good conversation, a thoughtful garden—whatever the style—shouldn't skip opportunities for unexpected delight. A touch of wit or whimsy here and there is punctuation for a garden's story, highlighting personalities of its creators and enhancing the joy for all who pass by.

GO FIGURE

Statuary of any kind, when used sparingly, adds unexpected flair and animation to the garden. Whether you choose a realistic animal sculpture or fantasy figure, be sure to place your statue in a quiet place in your garden and resist the urge to design around it or create an attention-grabbing shrine. The trick is to find a spot where the statue naturally fits instead of shouting "Here I am!"

LIVING GATES

If you love the look of vertical gardening but don't have much room, turn your garden gate into a living wall, with sun-loving succulents on one side and moss on the other. Here's how.

1 GRAB A GATE. The basic foundation for a living gate can be a variety of existing gates, or a custom-designed framework. Rustic, wooden gates fashioned from a frame of lumber (such as the one shown) work perfectly. Look for a funky window from a local salvage shop, antique store or thrift shop to add a little whimsy to your gate. Natural-looking "windows" can also be incorporated by way of cedar rounds from a hollow log.

2 HANG OUT. To use an existing wooden or metal gate, simply attach hanging pots and small windowboxes to the flat vertical surfaces using wire, screws, clamps and L-brackets. Or, fit and attach a few planted trays designed for a living wall to your existing gate.

3 MAKE A SANDWICH. To create the gate shown, construct two sets of a sturdy frame using reclaimed lumber cut to size. Sandwich growing medium between two layers of chicken wire, cut to fit and lined with fabric cloth. Then insert plants into cut openings.

ENGLISH LESSONS

The garden scene in the United Kingdom is as lush as it is legendary. A venerable Eden on earth, many of the grandest gardens in Devon and Cornwall were once private estates and manors. Now the grounds are open to the public, offering a wealth of garden wisdom and inspiration. On a tour, here are some simple lessons we took home.

GET GOOD BONES. Never an afterthought, hedges and walls are utilized brilliantly as major design features throughout the UK. This provides an essential framework and foundation for the garden.

DRAW THE EYE. Restraint is the key to creating a strong focal point. One or two key features only will pull the eye to signature sections of the garden; more will just confuse.

BEYOND THE ENGLISH ROSE. The Brits are actually not as hung up on roses as we think. More popular mainstays are heritage blooms such as *Crataegus* (hawthorn), and more contemporary selections such as *Cistus* (rock rose).

WONDERFUL WATTLE. Willow works feature prominently in English gardens, in the form of wattle fences and plant supports. Make your own by growing or collecting whips of English willow and weaving them in and out of assembled frames. You can make them as simple or as complex as you like.

A TASTE OF ITALY

We learned early how to adopt la dolce vita or "the sweet life" in the garden, Italian style. Italian gardens span the gamut, from the majesty of formal Renaissance-style spaces created for Roman nobility to the relaxed Tuscan manner of the countryside, celebrating life's simpler pleasures. For the home gardener, backyard Italian inspiration is easy to embrace—it's all about elegant surfaces and hardscaping, homegrown fare and everyday delights.

COURTYARD COURTSHIP. Fall in love with the intimacy and warmth of an Italian courtyard. Whether placed against the side of an existing building or designed as completely enclosed, the courtyard garden captures the sun and offers privacy, providing a warm enclave for heat-loving plants and a sweet spot to sit or stroll while soaking up the tranquil ambience.

AL FRESCO. The sweet life blooms in the garden with bountiful fruits, vegetables and herbs divided among dedicated plots and ornamental beds. Traditional Italian garden staples include garlic

and onions alongside succulent delicacies such as heritage tomatoes, zucchini and beans, figs, olives, plums, apples and cherries, plus such herbal delights as rosemary, oregano, basil and sage.

TERRA COTTA. Pot up a touch of Italy in terra cotta. The rich natural red of classic terra cotta (which literally means baked or cooked earth) instantly evokes a Tuscan mood.

AWESOME ACQUA. Water fountains and finial sculptures figure prominently in many Italian gardens. To stay on theme, opt for strong lines and architectural embellishments with your accessories.

SUPREMO STONE. Hardscaping Italian style includes ample placement of stone surfaces, paths, stacked or mortared walls and architectural features, as well as permanent ornamental stone sculptures. Whether you are building a palazzo patio, a stone garden shed or a simple rock wall around a herb bed, make it artful, robust and century-worthy (to last 100 years or more).

VINES TO VINO. You would be hard pressed to find an Italian garden without a grapevine or two. And it's remarkably easy to find the room. Just look up! Grow grapes and other vines on wooden trellises or arbours, or between two posts along strong wire. Supplement your crop with purchased grapes and you could even craft a batch of homemade Italian wine!

GARDENING BY THE SEA

Lucky are the few who get to garden by the sea! From rocky outcrops to sandy shores, the ample light and fresh breeze set a crisp tone while the glistening, steel-blue sea provides a stunning backdrop for the colour and textures of a coastal garden. But as soothing as it sounds, seaside gardening can be a challenge, especially when you factor in stormy coastal weather conditions. The salt, sun and wind that come with the territory can take a toll on tender plants and even the hardiest of gardeners.

SALT CHUCK. While some plants tolerate salty sea air quite well, others react dramatically as though it was a spritz of herbicide. The white film that results from ocean spray triggers moisture loss from leaves, causing some plants to wilt and deteriorate immediately or over time. While tough-stemmed plants, grasses and evergreens seem to possess a natural defence against sea spray, very few plants can take a repeated heavy dosing of seawater. Choose plants for

ocean-breeze tolerance and be sure any garden bed or container plantings are positioned well back from the surf and tidal zones, especially during the stormy winter season.

SOLAR POWER. Warm sunshine bouncing off crystal waters and abundant light make gardening near the ocean a special treat. But turn your back and these friendly seaside elements can quickly become rogue pirates, robbing your garden plants and soil of much-needed moisture. Unless your property is amply shaded by ornamental trees or natural forest, plan your garden accordingly to handle the full intensity of the seaside sun.

STORMS AND SURGES. Pink sky in the morning, gardeners take warning—a storm may be on its way. Along with chilling winds, storm surges are waves that crash up and over the tidal zone. If the resulting pull of surf doesn't uproot plants and trees completely, the flush of seawater can kill them. Wind causes limb breakage and dehydration in plants. It also carries salty sand, which may be deposited in garden beds. Support seaside plants and trees with stakes and trellising. And create your own microclimates by planting strong protective trees or erecting fences or walls to capture the best seaside qualities while keeping salty gusts and sea spray out.

Opposite: Seathrift, *Armeria maritima*; lupin, *Lupinus* sp.; sea holly, *Eryngium tripartitum*; West Coast wild flower mix

30 SEAWORTHY PLANTS

When choosing plants, look for those identified as sea tolerant first. Next, hardy, drought-tolerant plants are generally good choices. As a starting place, here is our favourite selection of seaworthy plants.

- Beach pea (*Lathyrus japonicus*)
- California lilac (*Ceonothus* spp.)
- Common thrift or sea pink (*Armeria maritima*)
- Crocosmia (*Crocosmia montbretia*)
- Dunegrass (*Elymus mollis*)
- English oak (*Quercus robur*)
- Foxglove (*Digitalis purpurea*)
- Foxtail lily (*Eremurus robustus*)
- Globe thistle (*Echinops*)
- Heather (*Calluna vulgaris*)
- Hebe (*Hebe* 'Patty's Purple')
- Honeysuckle (*Lonicera ciliosa*)
- Houseleek or hen and chicks (*Sempervivum*)
- Kinnikinnick or bearberry (*Arctostaphylos uva-ursi*)
- Laburnum (*Laburnum anagyroides* and *L.* × *watereri*)
- Maiden grass (*Miscanthus sinensis* 'Gracillimus')
- Mallow (*Lavatera* spp.)
- Oceanspray (*Holodiscus discolor*)
- Oregon grape (*Mahonia aquifolium*)
- Oriental poppy (*Papaver orientale*)
- Purple coneflower (*Echinacea purpurea*)
- Russell lupine (*Lupinus polyphyllus*)
- Russian olive (*Elaeagnus augustifolia*)
- Russian sage (*Perovskia atriplicifolia*)
- Salal (*Gaultheria shallon*)
- Saltspray rose (*Rosa rugosa*)
- Saskatoon berry (*Amelanchier alnifolia*)
- Sea holly (*Eryngium planum*)
- Sea urchin blue fescue (*Festuca glauca* 'Sea Urchin')
- Sequoia (*Sequoiadendron giganteum* and *S. sempervirens*)
- Tree lupine (*Lupinus arboreus*)

WATER WORKS

Make water a part of your garden. Save it for a sunny day, catch it in a swale garden, make a chain drain, sink and swim in it, plant up a pond, or simply capture the feel of flow with a river of stones or sedums.

SAVE WATER. With water shortages more and more an issue, gardeners now routinely look for ways to capture rain from roofs and other surfaces. Simple to sophisticated systems using plastic barrels or cisterns work well—once collected, water is pumped out to irrigate surrounding gardens or to supply ponds. An easy way to collect water for a small garden is to install a reservoir, such as a rain barrel, at the end of a down pipe. This basic level of water capture should be a priority in any sustainably designed landscape.

DIG A RAIN GARDEN. And another traditional method of water management is coming back into fashion. Rain gardens (open swales or low ditches) can curve along a roadway, driveway or walkway to slowly soak up water runoff from the neighbouring non-permeable surface.

ADD WATER-EVOCATIVE PLANTS. Many gardens have little space for an actual water feature. Yet, plants that emulate the seascape may add a sense of flow in the landscape. Consider swaths of grasses and patches of sedums.

STREAM AHEAD. If you have a large number of smaller round boulders on your property, try creating a dry or wet streambed. These are best located where you need to direct potential runoff from nearby driveways, downspouts or the low spot of a pond.

CHAIN SOME RAIN. Replacing a common downspout with decorative copper or contemporary steel rain chain is an excellent way to add a simple yet functional water feature. As rooftop runoff cascades down the chain, the sound and flow has a soothing effect. The water can be collected for use in the garden.

MAKE A STREAM A DREAM. For those lucky enough to have a small creek or flowing drainage ditch within their landscape, there is an opportunity for a wonderful showpiece. Small waterways, streams or swales can become a focal point if they flow through a garden or alongside a driveway, especially when enhanced by a bench or plantings.

USE AN OUTCROP. Your landscape may offer a natural rock outcrop from which you can create a simple water feature. To do so, you will need a small collection/re-circulating receptacle at the bottom (as your water source) and a pump with a well-hidden tube to snake the water back up to the outcrop.

ACT NATURAL. Garden ponds are traditionally built with rubber liners, concrete and clay and spray-foam surfaces. Be sensitive to the edges and keep everything as clean and simple as possible. When installing a liner, ensure that it will be invisible when the pond is filled or the result will be unsightly. Frame the edge of your pond with natural stone and rocks to soften it, but resist lining up similar-sized rocks uniformly. Mix up the scale just like Mother Nature does and use the stones to hide the liner material beneath any overhangs, bridges or submerged logs added to protect fish from predators.

MAKE A MOVE. The ultimate water garden invites movement so ensure there is motion—water may cascade, fish splash or reeds and lilies might sway in the wind.

DIVE IN. Swimming pools have always been popular and nowadays can be installed sustainably. An amazing design feature in a seaside landscape is a serene infinity pool with an edgeless effect. It can be framed by beautiful plantings or stonescapes that fit into the surrounding gardens or landscape. Alternatively, now common in Europe, new-age swimming pools are designed to look and live like a typical countryside pond. Planted and filtered naturally, these sustainable pools come complete with waterlilies and dragonflies, offering swimmers the rush of sinking into nature. Or, smaller scale pools sanitized with salt water can be situated in an open location that is prime for easy solar heating.

CURB APPEAL

There are a number of ways to improve the curb appeal of any yard. And, as a bonus, you'll add value to your property if you ever want to put it on the market!

BENCH IT. Consider adding a bench to the perimeter of your property—your neighbours will love the opportunity to sit and visit. Just remember to keep it well back from passing traffic. See page 155 for bench ideas.

ADD AN OUTLINE. Another inviting gesture is to create a small section of pathway along a boulevard. This will allow pedestrians to get off the road or shoulder to walk along a short, safe section of trail. Use materials like crusher dust, bark mulch or concrete pavers to carve out your path.

GET FRAMED. Try to plant as many trees as possible to frame your property or garden, especially on the street side. When a roadway is lined with mature trees, property values increase.

BRANCH OUT. If you are looking for new garden space, take advantage of off-street features such as a ditch or swale, which can often be planted up. Finding ways to hang flowering baskets and planters along property edges will also extend your garden space potential.

GET LIT

In the case of landscape lighting, less is more. Just a few effective choices can make pathways safe and your yard appealing even after the sun drops down. Plus, you can illuminate key elements—turning a tree cluster, water feature or rocky outcrop into a work of art.

LED. Modern LED technology has redefined outdoor lighting, offering substantial energy savings compared to traditional lighting options and longer-life bulbs. It costs a little more, but LED lighting is a worthwhile investment for main features in the garden and primary paths.

GO SOLAR. Compared to traditional outdoor lighting, solar LED lights are more flexible and easier to install, requiring no wiring and hence no trenches. Simply stake them into the ground and move them around to your heart's content.

LOW GLOW. Low-voltage "place and plug" outdoor landscape lighting is also safe, simple and relatively inexpensive. Use a spotlight to let a garden feature shine, or line a pathway to enable visitors to safely find their way to the front door. New improved shielded outdoor lighting fixtures also significantly reduce glare to help preserve the beauty of night skies.

FLAGSTONE UNDERFOOT

When considering materials for a deck, patio, driveway or front entry, weigh your options carefully. Sometimes the best approach is not the obvious one. For example, often people rely on one choice only for an entire space, but a great pairing is to match up flagstone pavers with concrete slabs. Natural flagstone also blends well with local landscape rock or any outcroppings you might happen to have on your property.

USE STOPGAPS. Installing stone in your landscape is relatively easy and presents endless opportunities. Simply outline your patio space and place the stones on a sturdy level surface, filling gaps with soil. If you like, you can also fill spaces with step-able plants such as creeping thyme. Or, use lawn, small stones, moss (from a sustainable source in your yard) or mortar. To mix things up a bit, try pairing giant flagstones with tumbled manufactured pavers in a simple pattern. We love the grey tones such as charcoal or pewter.

SAFE LANDING. If a front-door landing is required, use the largest flagstone piece as a non-slip, perfectly level entrance. Carry this further and utilize the same flagstone as treads for steps, combined with natural granite risers. Or try a stone threesome: natural granite landscape rock, large flagstone and tumbled pavers.

STAY LEVEL. To prep for flagstone or pavers in a path or patio, adjust any slope to allow for correct drainage, then firm up the base using materials such as yard scrapings. Time spent getting the surface level and compacted will ensure installation goes smoothly.

BRING IN HELP. To avoid wasting effort moving materials, plan to have stone delivered as close as possible to where it will be installed. You'll need several helpers to haul larger flagstone. A stone cutter may also be called for to custom fit pieces into a path or patio, along with a compactor to ensure pavers lie snugly on the ground. Ensure there are no gaps below the stone and that it does not rock when walked on.

BENCHMARKS

A garden is the loveliest setting to place benches for resting, enjoying landscape views or simply engaging in quiet contemplation. From classic and memorial park benches to formal ceremonial seats and every style in between, there is a bench suitable for any garden, guaranteed.

MATERIALS MATTER. When crafting or selecting outdoor garden benches, pay special attention to materials and seat height. Materials should be sturdy and weather resistant, such as sealed or oiled teak, cedar and fir, wrought iron or stone. Height and comfort will be variable depending on whether the bench is intended for children or adults. Most standard bench seats are 18 to 20 in. (45 to 50 cm) from the ground. If you like to swing your feet as you contemplate your garden, make your seat a little higher!

HARD AS ROCK. Gardeners of a sturdy disposition will be drawn to a simple granite bench. It requires just three stones: two strong supports for the base and a slab or lengthwise chunk for the top. The trick to making this bench is to keep it short and squat and to choose stones that naturally fit well together. The slab top is simply positioned on the two base stones and left to settle naturally. Sink the base stones into the ground slightly to increase stability. Test the slab for "toppleness." It should not move or wobble. If it slips or if the top and base don't fit together perfectly, use construction adhesive or special stone glue to fix the top to the base and fill in any gaps between them. Use caution when lifting and positioning heavy objects such as stone and be sure they are absolutely secure before leaving unattended.

RUSTIC TOUCH. Found driftwood and other sturdy slabs or base-worthy objects can be fashioned into simple seats. Our rustic bench is made from a fir timber, reclaimed from a dismantled factory. One length of timber was cut into three pieces. The two base pieces were cemented into the ground and the top timber attached with heavy-duty bolts, sunk deep into the top so they do not protrude above the seat. Before attaching the top timber, the surface was planed and sanded to create a contrasting face to the worn texture of the wood. Tung oil was applied to protect the original character, but the bench will continue to weather naturally.

STICKS AND STONES. Carefully placed boulders are a popular feature in many gardens. This bench plays off that theme with simple beauty and utility. Two large, flat-topped boulders are placed approximately 4 ft. (120 cm) apart and allowed to settle into the ground for several weeks. A plank of cedar is sized and cut to fit the width and length, then bolted into the stone with rods. This bench takes skill and care, as the boulders and plank must be prepared by drilling with a special tool that can penetrate stone (available at most tool-rental outlets). The threaded rods are ½ in. (1 cm) in varied lengths, and rock mortar is applied prior to drilling into the boulder. The rods are countersunk into the plank and a wooden plug is fashioned to create a seamless surface on top.

MODERN MUSE. Contemporary gardens have strong lines, and benches for these spaces need to be equally clean and spare in design. Our cedar bench is simply a long rectangle, 20 in. (50 cm) high by approximately 18 in. (45 cm) deep by 8 ft. (2.4 m) long. It was custom-milled from a cedar log that was deemed unfit for lumber production. While not many gardeners will have the tools to fashion such a bench at home, the clean lines may be mimicked with stacks of beams to create a long, lean seating structure, or you can custom-order a cut length of log from a mill.

FABULOUS FENCES

Whether you're defending your dahlias from deer, creating a safe space for children, penning in pets, protecting your privacy or simply defining your property's lines, there's no reason why your fence can't have style.

COMMON OR CUSTOM? Ready-made fencing panels are easy to install and come in various heights and sizes. For those with a little more time, however, a custom approach can add character. Driftwood-inspired fences constructed with hand-split cedar shakes instead of processed 1x6 cedar are appealing options. You can run the shakes vertically or horizontally, stain them, or leave them to naturally silver.

ADD CHARACTER. If you install a purely practical fence, such as one made of wire, soften the look and add personality with the addition of accents like birdhouses, beach logs (as posts) or top rails. Or insert a custom gate or decorative section.

LIVING FENCES. Instead of using a light-gauge trellis as fencing, consider a single or series of heavy cedar panels, made to fit any size opening and perfect for heavy climbers like Virginia creeper. Espaliered fruit trees can also be trained into an edible fence pattern. Wattle, live willow or living bamboo groves and hedges also make effective fences.

Gorgeous Gazebo

Got room for a gazebo? Traditionally gazebos were octagonal wooden structures placed in estate gardens as a public or private pavilion from which to take in the scenery or enjoy a pot of tea. Today, gazebos come in many shapes and materials to suit a wide selection of tastes, needs and budgets.

CUSTOM BUILT

There are gazebos for gazing, teahouse gazebos, log or canvas gazebos and even hot-tub gazebos to provide steamy shelter.

KIT PICK

Traditional wooden gazebo kits are extremely popular, very attractive and much longer lasting than their canvas counterparts. Kits are customizable and include everything you need to build a gazebo with limited carpentry skills. Prices for full-fledged wooden gazebo kits start at several thousand dollars and up.

DIY

But for a lot less, for those who prefer to work from scratch, pick out a gazebo plan and roll up your sleeves. It's easier than you might think.

GARDEN BAR

In the backyard or on the beach, a simple, old-fashioned tiki-style bar has enough character to become a focal point in your landscape.

1 **MAKE IT FIT.** Design and build your outdoor bar to suit your garden style. *Gilligan's Island* is not likely the look and feel you're after, but don't get too fancy either. Keep it rustic and simple, and consider local wood and stone for your foundation, structure and stools.

2 **SHAKE IT OUT.** Be sure to include a roof with a wide overhang for protection from showers. Hand-split five- or six-foot cedar shakes are ideal for a curved and twisted roof, while beach logs or rough-cut cedar with live (unfinished) edges make a wonderful countertop as would natural stone. Stools may be collected for your bar, or crafted from beach logs or rough-cut lumber.

3 **SET A GLOW.** If you have access to power or water lines, extend them to your bar area for convenient access and festive lighting. Or, you can install solar lighting and use a water dispenser.

4 **ACCESSORIZE.** Some cool accents for your garden bar might include a nearby dry-stack stone firepit, a water feature, local artisan sculpture or a beach-log bench. An attractive boardwalk or paver pathway leading from the barbecue area to bar, beach or backyard is a useful and striking addition.

Should Have Gnome

It's true that many a formal gardener wouldn't dream of adding the likes of a garden gnome to their prized plant collections. But let's admit it—the devilish little creatures do possess a certain rustic charm. Perhaps because of their diminutive size, children take special delight in their magical appearances in the garden, and they can cajole a smile out of the most uptight adult. Tuck a gnome under a shrub today, wrap one up as a gift for a gardener friend or, better yet, craft a miniature woodsy home for a family of gnomes. If you have the good fortune to have a backyard tree stump, simply add a small wooden door and window for your gnomes to call their own.

PERFECT PLAYHOUSE

There are many ways to create special features in your garden and a playhouse is the perfect place to start. Visiting grandchildren or your own kids will appreciate this unique retreat. A sturdy playhouse can also become a giant sleeping cabana in the summer and a handy haven during inclement weather.

ADD CHARACTER TO A KIT. Perhaps the quickest way to construct a playhouse is to buy a kit or shed and customize it. You can give soul to a prefab structure by using local and recycled materials as funky accents—think antique windows, custom benches and driftwood windowsills.

OR START FROM SCRATCH. Design something yourself, even making it up as you go along. Keep the scale modest and follow municipal guidelines if necessary, but also have fun. Plan a fort with flair—perhaps with a tree growing through the roof, a pirate flag or a spiral staircase.

USE WHAT'S THERE. Before you build, look at existing structures to see if you can add to them. A stump or tree could serve as a centre post. A rock outcrop complete with ferns may be used as a back wall. A ditch can become a funky watercourse, especially when complete with drawbridge.

LIVEN IT UP. An expanse of lawn surely needs to be broken up by something entertaining. Consider a live willow tunnel or a corn maze leading to the playhouse entrance. Sometimes these living features can become the playhouse, too. Sunflower huts and bean teepees make fabulous summer fortresses for kids.

GIVE IT NEW PURPOSE. When the children are grown, a thoughtful playhouse can do double duty and become an adult gathering spot for happy hour, a handy shed or a chicken coop.

Bamboo, *Phyllostachys bambusoides*

GROOVY GROVE

Bamboo—a tremendous resource for flooring, cabinets and countertops due to its strong, sustainable qualities—is also awesome to grow in the garden. From a simple potted clump to a long-stemmed forest, most landscapes benefit from bamboo.

PICK IT. With funky cultivars like 'Buddha's Belly', there are hundreds of available species of bamboo originating from Africa, Asia, and Central and South America. Giant timber bamboo reaches a height of 60 ft. (18 m) or more, while other species offer a wide range of size, colour and vivid variegation.

PLANT IT. A bamboo grove is super easy to design and install. Bamboo prefers full sun and loamy soil, but will adapt to a variety of conditions. Simply plant your bamboo in a row, repeating this to achieve the breadth of planting desired. Mulch well and water regularly until established.

SPREAD IT. Bamboo expands rapidly—even a few clumps can quickly thicken into a grove. It requires little maintenance and easily chokes out invasive weeds.

SEE AND HEAR IT. A bamboo grove offers acoustic benefits when the wind blows, as the long stems sway and rustle against each other. Add a water feature to weave through it for a tranquil and eye-catching enhancement. Because of its simplicity, a bamboo grove works especially well in contemporary landscapes. Add in a twisting path or a stone and timber bench for a Zen place.

WATCH IT. Bamboo is aggressive, so be careful not to plant it adjacent to perimeter drains, septic fields or delicate garden treasures. To be safe and deter bamboo's migration, consider using an underground rigid plastic barrier wall or liner around the patch to contain the bamboo so that you can enjoy its benefits without bother.

POT TRELLIS

*A pot trellis is a perfect small-scale experiment
from which to launch larger lattice handiwork.
Try making a variety of teeny trellises before
embarking on garden-size showpieces.*

1 First, make the arc by bending the top third of each upright into
a smooth curve. Fasten with wire against the opposite upright.

2 Next, fasten the centrepiece to the top of the arc. Shape one side
of the heart at a time, fastening carefully with wire. Use caution
when bending the heart curves as the branches will be prone to
breaking.

3 Finally, fasten the crosspiece at the base of the heart.

MATERIALS

Large pot

A selection of willow branches about ¼
in. (.75 cm) in diameter:

For the centerpiece, one 31-in.
(79-cm) branch

For the arch uprights, two 49-in.
(1.25-m) branches

For the heart, two 31½-in.
(80-cm) branches

For the crosspiece, one 16-in.
(40-cm) branch

GROW UP!

Running out of space in your garden? Grow up! Any vertical surface—a fence, rock wall, flagpole, tool-shed wall, stick teepee (ideal for scarlet runner beans) or even a tree trunk—can accommodate a garden or climbing vine.

GO TO THE WALL. Use vertical planters to transform a wall indoors or out into a garden. Purchase vertical plastic planters that can be suspended in a frame, or impermeable pockets for indoor use. You will often see these used in commercial situations but they work well in home gardens, too.

GET WIRED. Easier still, simply connect, suspend or hang cable, mesh or wire grid onto an exterior wall, fence or gate, and let your climbing plants and vines go wild.

STEP TO IT. Old ladders can become stairways to heaven when covered by roses, hops, grapes, sweet peas or clematis.

STACK IT UP. With supports you can grow squash, cucumbers, peas, tomatoes and hops up and over any available vertical surface. Or use a stacked container, planter or basket to allow easier access, or pile and plant up walls of stuffed landscape bags.

GOOD TIMES

Raise a glass to the garden! Chilling out with friends and family is our all-time favourite activity. It just makes sense to lay your shovel down from time to time and enjoy the fruits of your labour. A casual garden get-together is also a wonderful incentive to recruit helpers through the seasons. Who wouldn't pick a few buckets of apples for a share of sparkling cider a few months later? And making garden crafts is a great way to get the kids involved and stay dry on those inevitable rainy days. Just bring the garden inside!

FABULOUS FIGS

Rarely do we find a fruit this fabulous—equally sultry and simple. Imagine a classic comfort food that is also good for you. From snacks to gourmet accoutrements, figs are an unbeatable addition to your garden and table.

GROW

In mild areas, 'Black Mission,' 'Brown Turkey' and 'Desert King' have been shown to be quite productive. However, you'll need to place your fig tree in a spot where it receives full sun for the whole day in the summer for it to fruit consistently and for the fruit to ripen. Dwarf figs can even be grown in pots. This is especially handy if you live in a colder climate, as your fig may not be hardy enough to survive the winter. In a pot, you can simply drag it in for the winter.

EAT!

It's worth the extra effort to grow a few figs—if you've not tried them before, fresh figs can be a true culinary epiphany. Delicate, soft and subtle, the difference between a fresh and dried fig is somewhat akin to the distinction between a fresh grape and a raisin. Each taste

FIG JAM

You can use any kind of dried figs, but the dark, thin-skinned Mission figs offer the best texture.

INGREDIENTS

5 oz (150 gr)/1 cup (250 mL) dried figs, chopped finely (we use kitchen shears for this) with woody stems removed*

1 cup (250 mL) water

Zest and juice of ½ lemon

3 Tbsp/45 mL honey

METHOD

Place everything in a small saucepan and bring to a boil over medium heat. Reduce heat to minimum and simmer for 20 to 30 minutes (lid on), stirring occasionally until the figs are very soft. (Be careful not to scorch them and add more water if needed). Remove the lid and continue to simmer, until thick. Remove from heat, allow to cool and refrigerate.

Serve on crackers with goat cheese or soft blue cheese and a snip of lovely garnish from the garden. Special occasion? Drizzle the whole works with honey.

*Ripe, fresh figs will work too, but cut the water to ½ cup (125mL).

has its place, but real fig connoisseurs will rarely pass by a flat of these lush and juicy fresh delicacies. Also, fig leaves are handy when crafting serving platters. Use them to decoratively line plates and platters as you would grape leaves.

Figs are also packed with nutrition. They're fat free and provide 20 percent of our recommended daily fibre per serving. In addition, they are rich in potassium, calcium and iron. Fig purée is often used as a sweetener and fat replacement in baking.

1 Dry. Use a dehydrator to preserve your homegrown figs. Dried figs are delicious when eaten out of hand, sliced and added to goat-cheese salads, as an addition to a cheese tray, or cooked into compote.

2 Dessert. You can simmer a handful of dried figs for 10 minutes in ½ cup (125 mL) of brandy, with vanilla and honey to taste, for a wonderful winter accompaniment to ice cream.

3 Drizzle. Fresh figs may be eaten as is, halved and grilled, or drizzled with honey or maple syrup. And the taste of figs is sublime when paired with late-harvest white wines, such as Gewurztraminer and ice wines or ports.

HOT STALKS

Nothing heralds the arrival of spring quite like the tender shoots of an asparagus crop. And the soft snap of a perfectly cooked asparagus stem signals a taste experience that is healthful, delicious and decadent in its simplicity. At only five calories per average stem, you can eat a lot of asparagus without feeling guilty, plus it's a good source of vitamins A, B and C.

GROW

Asparagus is an "investment crop," meaning you must invest time and effort now for big returns later. But those tender stalks are worth it and, once established, an asparagus bed will produce for decades to come.

To plant asparagus, you'll need an empty or new soil bed with good drainage in full sun. Double-dig new areas and amend with compost and manure. Next, dig a trench at least 1 ft. (30 cm) wide by 5 ft. (1.5 m) long by 6 in. (15 cm) deep.

Purchase asparagus crowns from a local nursery. Crowns essentially look like roots with a central tip. They should be plump and robust-looking rather than dry. Plant them as directed in the trench, about 1 ft. (30 cm) apart, spreading the root tendrils out away from the higher crown. Cover the roots and crown with several inches of soil and tamp down. Over time, as the plants grow, fill in the trench entirely until it reaches ground level.

You may see asparagus stalks the first season. But here's the trick—don't pick them! The roots need time to develop and future crops depend on your leaving the first year's stalks alone. Once you hit year two, pick a handful or so. By year three, go for a bunch!

EAT!

When choosing asparagus at the market, we often reach for bunches with the thinnest stems. This yields the most tender shoots and mildest flavour when steamed. However, the thicker mature stems are also excellent for steaming and make the best choice for grilling or adding to salads, sandwiches or wraps.

1 STEAM. Cook your asparagus in a steamer tray over a large pot, or preferably in a single layer in an Asian bamboo steamer placed over a wok full of boiling water. Steam until the stem is just tender when pierced with a fork. Steamed asparagus is perfect exactly as is, especially when served with a few drops of virgin olive oil or a dab of fresh butter, a dash of salt and pepper, and a squeeze of fresh lemon juice.

2 STORE. You may also wish to save cooked asparagus as additions to other dishes. First, steam the stems until tender and then plunge into a bowl of very cold or ice water to stop the cooking process. Store the cooked, chilled asparagus in the refrigerator, and add it chopped to salads or pizza toppings, or line the stalks inside panini, wraps or sushi rolls.

3 SKEWER. Asparagus is also excellent on the grill. Just lightly steam or blanch the stalks, then thread the stems, end to end, through two skewers creating a raft. Or simply place your stalks in a grilling basket. Spray or brush with olive oil and grill until seared and tender, flipping once. Serve with a squeeze of lemon.

OLIVE AFFAIR

We love olives. Green or black, stuffed, chopped, pitted or not, we're always ready to toss them back like candy. What's more, while these salty gems taste sinfully rich, they're actually good for you. Relatively low in fat—the mono-unsaturated kind that has a beneficial effect on your body's cholesterol—they are also a good source of vitamin E and antioxidants, and contain just seven calories per large olive.

GROW

Olives traditionally grow on trees thriving in warmer climates such as the Mediterranean, but you can also grow small olive shrubs such as *Olea europaea* in milder climates (zones 8–10).

Select a site that's warm, high and dry. Choose small specimens (olives are a relatively new introduction to nursery stock so you'll likely find only young plants) as they are easiest to establish.

Sandy, well-drained, fertile soil is best. Fruit will appear in late summer and needs an extended warm period to ripen. Olives grow well against a sunny wall, protected from wind, rain and frost.

If you aren't confident your zone is warm enough, pot your olive shrub and treat it like citrus, bringing it indoors to winter. We keep our olive shrubs planted in a sunny spot outdoors year round.

EAT!

At about five years old, *Olea europaea* should produce a small crop that can be cured in brine and enjoyed in many ways.

1 **SOLO.** Savour the flavour of olives on their own. Simply serve them as a pre-dinner snack with a glass of wine or a cocktail. Don't forget a small bowl for the pits.

2 **SALAD.** Toss a handful of sliced olives into a chopped salad or pasta dish.

3 **SPREAD.** Make homemade olive tapenade by finely chopping a handful of pitted olives with a clove or two of garlic. Blend with a tablespoon of olive oil and a squeeze of fresh lemon juice. Season with salt and pepper and serve on crackers.

4 **SOAKED.** Marinate olives in mixed citrus rind (the rind of one organic orange and lemon sliced finely) with fresh rosemary and olive oil to cover. Let sit, covered, in the fridge for 24 hours before serving.

EDIBLE PETALS

For those of you who can't resist a pretty nibble, here are some tips to serving edible petals with tasteful restraint.

GROW

First an alert: not all flowers are edible! Buy your edible flowers and petals from a reputable grocer, or research them well before growing your own. Safest bets are culinary herb flowers like tangy rosemary and mild chive blossoms; or sunny calendula petals and peppery nasturtium leaves and petals. Bee balm, borage blossoms and violas round out the common offerings. When picking, purchasing or growing edible petals, avoid the use of any chemicals and seek out petals that are as fresh as possible. Carefully clean your flowers with cool water and pat to dry. Watch for bugs. . .

EAT!

1 SOLITARY REFINEMENT. A single edible flower makes a solid statement on a plate. Lone blossoms work best as a garnish to top a salad, set off the icing on a cupcake or grace the side of an entrée. But when serving flowers as part of a salad, it's best to carefully separate the petals or tiny blossoms first. Not only will a light sprinkling of petals taste better, the flowers will also go further. Try this with chive blossoms (too often tossed as a whole orb with abandon into salads). While the full blooms have a texture reminiscent of straw, when the cluster is separated, it turns into little lilac stars, each with a silky skin and delicate flavour.

2 FLOWER FLOAT. You can also freeze colourful petals or whole smaller blooms in ice-cube trays to add a dash of colour and glamour to cocktails, punch and lemonade. As the ice melts, the flowers will float to the surface and still look grand. You can also mix in chopped aromatic blooms such as lavender to flavour ice creams and frozen treats.

3 SUGAR SWEET. Make candied petals and blooms from tiny edible roses or petals. Collect and clean the flowers, then brush them gently with a mixture of powdered egg white and water. Finally, dip the flowers in sugar. Allow them to dry and use to garnish sweets and cakes.

MATERIALS

Solar print paper (available at craft stores)

Shallow pan

Water

Garden leaves, flowers and more

INDIGO SUMMER

Want to have some creative fun in the sun? Make a solar photo! This special light-sensitive paper is designed to be used with solar rays. In striking blue and white contrast, the paper allows you to make prints from natural leaves, flowers and other objects in the sun. It's a great craft for kids and cool enough for adults as well.

1 Solar print paper is usually stored in black plastic to keep light from hitting the surface until you are ready to print. It's important to refrain from exposing each sheet to light until you have gathered all your materials.

2 Collect some flat objects that will fit within the dimensions of your paper. We used cut flowers and herbs from the garden. Seed pods, twigs and stones also work well.

3 Remove one sheet of paper and lay it on a sturdy flat surface, blue side up. Quickly and carefully arrange your objects on the paper. Then, place the paper with objects in the sun for a few minutes until the paper turns white. Try not to move the objects or your print will be blurry.

4 Once fully exposed, bring the paper inside and rinse the print in a shallow pan of tap water. Dry your print flat, then frame and display. Beautiful!

HELLO KITTY

We are so lucky to have a large French pussy willow (Salix caprea) in our front yard. Such a cheery sight in late winter when the catkins (the fuzzy bits) start to swell. The tree grows like a weed and takes to pruning very well. As such, it is a great supplier of stems to display, share and even occasionally sell to florists. And you can also take cuttings to create more pussy willow shrubs.

1 **GROW IT.** Willow is extremely easy to propagate. Basically, you can just cut a stem and stick it in the ground during early spring. If the conditions are right and it stays wet enough, the cutting will easily start to root and grow into a small whip, then a stringy shrub. . . and soon you'll have a pussy willow tree.

2 **SHOW IT.** As for the cut pussy willow stems, sometimes we like to go with a minimal Zen-like display, using one or two stems in a pretty vase. Other times, we try to be a bit more modern, using a glass container and more graphic presentation. Either way, you can't help but be amazed at how soft those little puffballs are.

MATERIALS

One large sunflower

Chicken wire or laundry rack

Decorative natural materials such as dried leaves and flowers

Wire

SUNFLOWER SEEDER

Everyone enjoys the bright sunny face of sunflowers. And the magic doesn't have to end once the blooms lose their colour and begin to droop in late autumn. Pick them before they fall and fashion the dried sunflower heads into decorative birdfeeders to delight your feathered friends.

1 To make the feeder you'll need a mature sunflower head. By late September through October, seeds should be fully visible and most of the petals wilted or dry. Pick the head and allow it to air dry in a warm place, ideally lying flat on a suspended bed of chicken wire (stem through the wire) or a portable laundry rack. When the back of the flower head is no longer green and the entire head feels light and dry you are ready to begin.

2 Collect a variety of decorative natural materials including cornhusks, dried leaves, flowers and seed pods. Use a glue gun to attach the decorative elements to the sunflower head. Or leave your sunflower plain for an "au natural" look.

3 Create a hanger by piercing the side of the head, stringing the wire through to the other side (approximately 5 in./13 cm apart) and fastening a loop.

4 Hang in a protected area, preferably below an overhang and away from the reach of predators. Birds will cling to the flower head and happily pick at the seeds, just like in nature. Unlike manufactured feeders, less seed will be flung around and wasted too.

INGREDIENTS

4 cups (1 litre) fresh chopped rhubarb

½ cup (125 mL) granulated sugar

½ cup (125 mL) water

Juice of 1 lemon

RHUBARB LEMONADE

A splash of rhubarb syrup or compote adds a tart tang and cheeky pink tinge to an otherwise ordinary drink. We like to mix it with our classic lemonade or an inexpensive sparkling wine. Adding an ounce or two of vodka will take your rhubarb drink to the next level, if you know what we mean.

1 Place rhubarb in a pot. Then add ½ cup (125 mL) granulated sugar (or more if you like it sweeter) and ½ cup (125 mL) water, plus the juice of 1 lemon (optional, to extend the colour if you are saving the syrup for later).

2 Bring the rhubarb mixture to a low simmer, stirring to prevent scorching. Cook your rhubarb until soft, making a nice compote.

3 Then strain the compote using a sieve or loosely woven cheesecloth, allowing the syrupy liquid to collect in a large bowl.

4 Pour the syrup into a bottle and store in the refrigerator.

5 Use the remaining pulp for loaves or muffins, or compost it.

6 Once you've made your rhubarb syrup, when the mood strikes, simply add a spoonful to your lemonade or other drinks. Stir and enjoy!

TIP: You can skip straining your compote into syrup if you are lazy or don't mind a heavier drink (just give it a cool name like Pulp Fiction). Either way, delicious.

HERE COMES THE SUN

What a charming way to end a day in the garden—sit back, relax and enjoy a sip of freshly brewed sun tea. Over ice, with lemon and fresh mint, sun tea is refreshingly easy to make and lovely to serve. With just a little preparation, a handful of ingredients and the energy of the sun, you and your guests will be basking in the glow in no time.

INGREDIENTS

8 cups (2 litres) cold water

2–4 teabags (optional)

1–2 cups (250–500 mL) chopped herbs

Lemon wedges

Edible flowers (optional)

Honey or sugar

1 You'll need a large, clean glass jar with a lid. Stuff it one quarter full of fresh-cut washed organic herbs (peppermint, bee balm, lemon balm, chamomile, sage, basil). The combinations are endless, so experiment, but keep your selections to two or three herbs at a time. You can also add black, green or herbal teabags if you desire.

2 Fill the jar with clear, cold water. Cover and place in the sun for approximately three hours.

3 Once brewed to taste, strain and add liquid honey, agave or maple syrup to sweeten. Chill and serve on ice with lemon and an edible flower-petal garnish. Enjoy—it's like sipping sunshine!

GOODTIME GARDEN SIPS

Backyard trends may come and go, but celebrations featuring delicious food and drink made from garden-fresh ingredients will always be in style—and for a very good reason. Creating meals from homegrown fruits and vegetables is a beautiful multi-layered experience, from the planting to the picking to the preparing and presentation. And making soft or hard drinks from ingredients plucked from our own gardens is equally memorable.

HOP TO IT. For the beer drinker, try growing your own aromatic hops to supplement beer recipes or kits. Plant a hop (*Humulus lupulus*) in any spot suitable for an ornamental climber. Fasten wires to an unsightly service pole for the hop vines to twist up and around. A vertical garden using multiple stainless-steel cables securely adhered to a sunny wall will allow hops to spread up and out. Or try using slender cedar, beach or willow poles to create a simple teepee—your hops will quickly turn it into a golden tower.

Hop vines can also cover an ugly fenceline. Every chainlink fence on the block could be used to host a hop! Better beer-making is a nice bonus from growing these beautiful vines!

Hops desire a moist organically rich soil. To grow them well, provide the same compost, mulch and water you would for any other vigorous climber.

Once the hops are mature, pick and allow the mature female flowers to fully dry before storing for later use. Most people nowadays like to use ready-to-go beer kits to make home brew. You can fortify the flavour of a kit by tossing in a couple of handfuls of your own homegrown hops to add an aromatic zest to any standard mix.

DIVINE WINE. A more common garden plant is the grape, both for table and wine. Red and white grapevines in dozens of varieties are readily available and beautiful to look at throughout the year. Heavily pruned, they have a sculptural quality in the dead of winter, are lush in spring and succulently laden with grapes by late summer. Even non-wine drinkers will appreciate freshly squeezed grape juice or a delicious bunch for lunch.

To grow grapes at home, pick a well-exposed site where vines can climb into the sunshine. Let them swoop up and over an old cabin, shed or brush pile.

Winemakers traditionally rely on posts strung horizontally with wire to support grapevines. Simple split-rail cedar or cedar beach logs work well too. Try scorching the ends, or treat with oil those areas that will be in contact with the ground, then surround posts with well-drained rock to help them last longer.

Like most plants, grapevines enjoy plenty of compost, beneficial fungus, any organic amendments like leaf mould, sawdust, seaweed, fish fertilizer, bone and bloodmeal. An organic fertilizer applied on the surface will also optimize growth, as will providing a soothing layer of organic mulch to help moderate temperature, retain moisture and host beneficial organisms.

Grapes prefer well-drained soil. Ideally, the surrounding area is sloped and made up of suitable, well-drained or sandy growing medium. Dig a square hole, carefully plant your wine or table grapevines, and train them around their supports. Then sit back and wait—once you have two to three pounds of grapes, you've got enough for a gallon of wine!

SUPERB CIDER. Making both hard and soft cider is a very old tradition. There are literally hundreds of varieties of cider-worthy apples available for you to grow. Consider growing early- and late-harvest crops to extend the cider season. Blending a combination of apple juices can allow you to experiment and test the delicious results on your friends and family. Don't forget to try adding tart crabapples to the mix.

Keep your eye out for traditional cider-making apples, usually among the sharp or bittersharp or bittersweet varieties. Most apples that are not considered great for eating are excellent candidates for a cider grove. On narrow vertical surfaces such as your fence or along a garden path, train your trees into a space-saving espaliered form.

To make cider, you'll need an orchard ladder for picking, as well as boxes for storing, a hose for washing up, work table, cutting board and knife, a crusher and grinder, apple press, several clean buckets and finally carboys for fermenting and storage.

Once you press your apple juice, you'll need to decide whether you wish to make hard (alcoholic) or soft (juice) cider. Consult books for proper fermentation, pasteurization and storage tips. Making a little of both kinds of cider is the best—one to enjoy right after harvest, the other to store and savour at a later date.

COOL FAVOURS

When the heat is on, party planners need to keep the mood extra cool. These frozen summer party favours will delight your guests and let everyone else know that the fun is officially happening: time to chill out, people!

FANCY CUBES. Why be square? Pick up some fanciful shaped ice-cube trays (think stars, hearts and flowers) and freeze away. Use juice, lemonade or iced tea in your ice-cube trays for colourful fruit-cocktail ice. Got an ice-cube machine in your fridge already? That's great. Just freeze a few dozen of the shaped cubes and mix them into your supply of regular ice cubes.

ICED SHOOTERS. Want that next shot of vodka to be extra cool and super pretty? Serve your tray of party shooters in frozen "ice" glasses infused with flowers and herbs. You can simply use a pair of plastic cups—one medium, one small—as a mould. To make with cups, use tape and a bit of cardboard to hold the small cup inside the bigger cup with an air space all around and in between. Fill the space with water and insert herbs and flowers. Place in the freezer. Once frozen, run the cups under warm water until they release.

BERRY SWIZZLE. Serving sangria or another fruity cocktail? Make frozen cocktail swizzle sticks and cause a stir! Thread berries and small chunks of fruit onto medium bamboo skewers. Keep the amount of fruit consistent with the height of your cocktail glass. Freeze in a single layer and keep in the freezer until needed. After mixing, place one swizzle stick into each cocktail prior to serving.

INGREDIENTS

4 cups (1 litre) fresh chopped rhubarb

4 cups (1 litre) (approximately) chopped red apples or crabapples; remove stems but no need to core

1 cup (250 mL) sugar

2–3 cups (500–750 mL) vodka

Juice of ½ lemon

Slices from ½ lemon

APPLE ELIXIR

No time to make wine, beer or cider from scratch? Try this little vixen instead. Our apple elixir is a favourite potion as well, mostly because it is so easy to make and even easier to drink.

1 Place apples and lemon slices in a jar (fill to the top), then add the lemon juice and sugar.

2 Fill the jar to the rim with vodka.

3 Screw on the lid and put in a dark place for two to three weeks.

4 Decant the infusion by straining the mixture through cheesecloth. Enjoy over ice or mixed with sparkling water.

MATERIALS

Ripe, washed fruit of your choice

Pastry brush

Honey

Olive or grapeseed oil

GRILLING FRUIT

It may not be the first thing that comes to mind when you think of barbecuing, but grilled fruit is an awesome addition to your summer repertoire.

Try some mixed grilled fruits on a salad, as burger toppings, or as a sweet and simple dessert. Rhubarb, plums and peaches are awesome when cooked on the grill and apples turn into candy. In fact, once you start grilling fruit, the only danger is that you may never go back to plain old fruit salad again.

Start with good-quality ripe fruits. Unripe fruits will only stay hard and taste unsatisfying. Peaches, nectarines, apricots and plums should be left unpeeled, but washed, cored and cut in half. Brush with oil and grill for one minute over medium heat, skin-side down first. Flip and grill until soft and caramelized. These fruits taste wonderful when grilled and served warm with vanilla ice cream or plain yogourt.

Apples and pears may also be grilled (halved, cored, peeled or unpeeled), however, it helps to poach them slightly first to cut the grilling/cooking time. Brush the poached halves with oil and grill for two minutes on each side. Awesome as a dessert or a warm salad topping.

Mixed fruit skewers are fun to grill as well. Cut the fruit into 1-in. (2.5-cm) pieces, thread on a bamboo skewer, brush with oil and grill for a minute on each side. If you're short on time, purchase fresh-cut fruit salad. Try adding pitted cherries and grapes to your mix.

To grill rhubarb, drizzle fresh, clean stalks with honey and olive oil. Sear on a hot grill (use tongs), then cook for a few minutes on low (lid down) until just barely soft. Chop the grilled pieces and serve warm over vanilla ice cream, plain Greek yogourt or vanilla custard. Drizzle with honey.

Hungarian wax peppers

Opposite: Thai dragon peppers

RED-HOT PEPPERS

Do you know your habanero from jalepeno? If you're flirting with growing fiery peppers in your garden, it helps to know just how hot to go.

GROW

To grow peppers successfully in a moderate or cool climate you will need a long hot summer. You can increase your success by growing peppers against a rock or stone wall, in black pots, in a hothouse or under solar cover. Buy peppers as seedlings to get a head start. They are moderate feeders and may require staking or caging to stand upright when heavy with fruit.

All hot or chili peppers contain capsaicin, the natural chemical that causes the sensation of heat on the tongue and in the mouth. Bell peppers don't contain capsaicin so grow them if you prefer a mild taste. Least searing of all, the chili peppers, pepperoncini and New Mexican peppers contain just a touch of sizzle. The more common jalapeno, wax and rocotillo peppers are hotter and good choices for most recipes calling for fresh-cut chilies. But they pale in comparison to red-hot Serrano, cayenne and Thai peppers. Topping the chili charts are the smallest peppers, including the infamous and colourful habanero peppers. You should only grow, prepare and eat these hot, hot, hot peppers in a very cautious manner.

The seeds and inside white thread-like area of chili peppers are the hottest. You can neutralize some of the capsaicin effect by removing the seeds and threads prior to chopping, cooking and consuming.

When handling very hot peppers, use gloves or wash your hands completely as soon as you are done. If you fail to do so and rub your eyes or nose, you will pay dearly for the indiscretion with a nasty burning sensation.

EAT!

FRESH. Eat fresh bell-type peppers on their own as a cut veggie, or in wraps, tacos and salads.

DRIED. Dry hot peppers in a dehydrator or simply air dry them by stringing small peppers with a needle and butcher twin. Hang in a cool dry place.

GRILLED. Sear on the barbecue to add a smoky flavour. Simply brush whole peppers with oil and grill until charred and soft. Placed the hot cooked peppers in a paper bag and allow to cool. The charred skins will then slip off and you can slice and enjoy the peppers.

HUNT AND GATHER

Here are a few fall accents you can easily create with materials around the home and garden. Freshen up your living space and enjoy a warmer, cheery décor with squash votives, a leafy wreath, napkin prints and more.

THINK SQUASH. We love those mini-pumpkins so popular right now. Pick up a bag and strew them around your living space for a lighthearted touch. Or pile them high in a pretty autumn basket at the centre of your table. You can also remove the tops, hollow out a small depression in the centre of the squash and fit a tealight inside to create a seasonal votive candleholder. Mini pumpkins also make great jack-o-lanterns.

GET POTTED. Garden pots aren't doing much outside this time of year. But they look great when turned into simple seasonal displays. Place two large pumpkins atop a pair of terra-cotta pots or urns and create a funky fall entranceway on your doorstep. Use an oversized empty cedar planter to house branches and firewood for your outdoor chiminea or fireplace. Or, greet guests at the door to your festive party by refashioning a large garden urn into a fabulous cooler.

COLLECT LEAVES. Pick up a collection of colourful fall leaves, press and dry them between sheets of newspaper, under books. Scatter the leaves on your fall dinner table, or affix them to a wreath form using a glue gun for stunningly easy fall display.

PRINT THEM. Those same leaves may be used to stamp impressions onto a fall tablecloth or set of paper or fabric serviettes. Simply brush a small amount of paint or fabric paint onto the surface of the leaf you wish to replicate. Press the leaf, painted side down, onto your fabric or selected surface, then carefully peel it away and allow the paint to dry.

PUMPKIN PERFECTION

Versatile, delicious and beautiful, you can do a whole lot more with pumpkins than carve them for Halloween. Plump and healthful, this colourful squash is packed with nutrition, fibre and, most of all, flavour.

Pumpkins and winter squash have been grown in North America for over 5,000 years, originally by Native Americans and later by European explorers. The common name "pumpkin" is said to come from the Greek word for "large melon" or "pepon." A creative American colonist is credited with inventing pumpkin pie by hollowing a squash, filling the cavity with cream, spices and molasses, and baking it on hot ashes left over from an open fire. Late-fall beach party, anyone?

GROW

Pumpkins come in many shapes and sizes and some are better suited to decorative or cooking uses than others. Try to grow a variety if you have the room, especially the funky heritage cultivars.

If space is at a premium in your garden, the smallest, decorative pumpkins are just the size of a fist. Combine them with some fall leaves and greenery to create a colourful centrepiece for your table. Or carve small holes in the tops of these tiny pumpkins to make perfect tealight candleholders.

EAT!

ROAST. Small sugar pumpkins are best for pie and tart filling, soups and baking. To roast the flesh of a sugar pumpkin, start with washing the outside of your pumpkin and then slice it open lengthwise. Scoop out the threadlike mass of seeds and then cut the flesh into triangular wedges. Roast on a cookie sheet, uncovered, in a 300F (150C) oven for 2 hours until the flesh is slightly caramelized and very soft and tender. Scoop the flesh away from the skin and mash. Use this creamy pumpkin base to make soups, pie fillings or baked goods. You can do this with larger pumpkins too, or use any orange-fleshed squash for recipes calling for pumpkin.

SCOOP FOR SOUP. Large pumpkins make terrific soup tureens. Just cut off the top in a circular fashion around the stem, lift and scoop out the innards, leaving a thick layer of flesh to protect the skin. Fill your tureen with cooked and heated soup or stew and carefully place on a serving tray at the table. French-styled heirloom pumpkins have flat, wheel-like shapes, perfect for stuffing with wild rice, apples and cheese. Clean, stuff, bake whole, and bring to the table for a stunning display at your next buffet.

SAVOUR THE SEEDS. Don't forget to save the seeds! Roasted pumpkin seeds are delicious, healthy and fun to prepare with kids. Before carving or roasting your pumpkin, scoop out all the seeds and separate from the thread-like flesh. Rinse well, cleaning as much pumpkin off each seed casing as possible. Roast whole in a 350F (175C) oven for 30 minutes. While hot, top with salt and other seasonings. To snack, split the pumpkin shell with your teeth or fingers and eat the seed within. Or, if you like the crunchy texture and want more fibre, eat the roasted shell too. Scrumptious!

MATERIALS

A pair of containers, one large, and one small, sized to fit the height of your candleholder as well as the width and height of your candle. We used a 2-quart (2-litre) plastic milk carton, a large yogourt container and a plastic condiment bottle.

Gorgeous garden greenery, rosehips, berries and seed heads

Candle

CANDLE ICE

Make these cool garden-inspired candles to light the way to your next wintertime party. They take just minutes to make (plus freezing time), and are guaranteed to set a warm glow on a chilly holiday evening.

1 Fill the larger container with about 1 in. (2.5 cm) of water. Place the container in the deep freeze on a flat surface and allow the base to freeze solid.

2 Remove from the freezer and place the smaller container (a candleholder is ideal) inside the larger one, resting it on the base of ice.

3 Tuck greenery, rosehips and small winter branches into the crevice between the containers and then fill this space with water right to the top. Place a heavy object inside the smaller container to prevent it from floating up.

4 Then carefully return the pair of containers to the freezer for at least 24 hours until the water freezes solid. To release the ice candleholder, remove the set from the freezer and allow to thaw just slightly, at room temperature. Or run the containers under warm water until the ice releases.

5 Set outside, insert candle, light and enjoy.

Tree Tip

Wondering which live tree to choose? Traditional holiday tree favourites are noble, balsam, Fraser and Douglas fir and Scots pine. But, frankly, any evergreen tree would be lovely!

CHRISTMAS TREE REDUX!

A fresh-cut or live tree from the nursery, tree-farm or seasonal tree supplier is a great way to set an old-fashioned tone for the holidays. Sometimes you can also obtain a small live tree to pot up or cut from a potential construction or development site.

CUT IT. Keep your fresh-cut tree well watered and located in a cool space in your home. At the end of the holidays, chip and compost your tree into beautiful mulch.

REUSE IT. A live tree will be a welcome addition to your garden after the holidays. Reusing the same tree for many years is also a great option. Keep your multi-year tree in a pot and plan to use it seasonally until it gets too big and heavy to bring inside, at which point you can plant it permanently into the ground.

SALVAGE IT. At construction sites, ask permission and most site supervisors will allow you to salvage a tree that will otherwise be destroyed. A small pull pruning saw and/or a shovel are all the tools you need. When you get home, store the cut tree in a cool, shady spot in water until it is time to move indoors. Pot up the live tree and take pride in the fact that you saved it from being squashed.

INDEX